ORDINARY CHAMPIONS

HOW TO ACHIEVE YOUR FULL POTENTIAL AND OUTPERFORM YOURSELF

MANOJ AGARWAL

PRAISE

"A very unique and useful perspective for those starting out and those on the ladder, interspersed with Manoj's very personal experiences that formed his thinking. I'm very happy to have worked with Manoj and pleased we remain friends."
    David Patterson, Programme Director

"A very honest and relatable look into the career world and how to get the most out of yourself. A great read, with many suggestions that I plan to act on for my own growth."
    Alex Fiorello, Solutions Architect

"If you don't feel fulfilled at work, reading this book could be your salvation. It is a quick and easy read yet has a step-wise plan which should enable you, with hard work & commitment, to formulate and then achieve your personal goals and ambitions."
    David Willcox, Project Management Consultant

"I think the book has everything one would need to create self-awareness about oneself, irrespective of what field you are into. The book has real life situations along with some wonderful quotes which one would feel more connected to. My favourite part is the section on fear, anybody can be a champion and focus on strengths. Overall the book is very good, a must read!!"
    Nitika Joshi - Project Manager

"This book is full of ideas and exercises for those wanting to get themselves out of a rut, or needing to make a step change – or as guidance for their managers. Manoj has used his own story to inspire the reader to overcome self-limiting beliefs and behaviours and along the way, there are timely reminders that success is built on repeated and focused effort. You will definitely find something here that you can use."

Judy Holliday, Director at People and Potential Ltd

"This is not a self-help book or a how-to guide for personal development. This book is nothing less than a manifesto, for showing the reader that they have means within to excel at their chosen goals. The author uses examples, case studies and personal experience to encourage self-reflection, and awareness of one's own abilities. The style is energizing, with a streak of humour, and some great narrative stories. The end result is a practical and entertaining read, with a great sense of personal challenge in each chapter."

Sean Jones, Lead Solutions Architect

"It is a refreshing, thought-provoking and inspiring book. I feel it has ignited my inner desire to pursue my forgotten dreams."

Ranjan Jha, Digital Design expert

"As human beings in the professional world, we all want to become the best in what we do but unfortunately only a handful are able to progress and become successful. The concept of "Ordinary champions" is such a unique and refreshing read which focuses on fundamentals of the reasons on what stops any and every ordinary person from becoming a champion and be successful in his or her field. It also provides such a simple method to unleash your potential and achieve greater success in whatever you pursue. In "Ordinary Champions", Manoj draws on his decades of experience bringing out the key insights on reasons which hold you back in excelling and also, more importantly, presents most powerful methods ever discovered for increasing the effectiveness of any individual or group. After a long time, I have come across a book which is such an easy and effective read and conveys such a powerful method, which if adopted, will definitely help any person achieve greater goals. I feel very motivated and enlightened after reading this great book."
Mohit Talwar, Chief Technology Officer

"This book resonated with my own feelings and thoughts, it is down to earth and straight from the gut. It touches your core and shakes you up. It compels you to go and do something and shape your own destiny."
Raushan K Choudhary, Joint Director, Ministry of Statistics & Program Implementation, Govt of India

DEDICATION

To all those who I shared the journey with.

All royalty payments from this book in any format, print, electronic, media and from all future productions related to this work will be donated to

The British Stammering Association.

LEAP. | Books

First published in Great Britain 2017 by Manoj Agarwal.

Illustrations and cartoons: David Willcox
Book Cover Design: Ranjan Jha

CONTENTS

MANOJ AGARWAL

PREFACE

The idea of writing this book came about during a chance encounter with Daniel Priestley, entrepreneur, best-selling author and international speaker. Daniel began by asking what do I do, why I do what I do and what makes me who I am. I was, frankly, struggling to answer the questions.

Shortly after, it started to unravel and it became clear that the key ingredients of my modest successes over the years have been transforming people, not technology.

We agreed that I will test the idea of the book with a core group of potential readers and research the subject. I will then summarise my experience of creating high performing teams and individuals in the form of a method and support it with real-life stories and anecdotes. Daniel also came up with the title "Ordinary Champions".

Today, our world is full of promise. The resources are plentiful and opportunities are endless. Traditional big players in the industry are being disrupted by students operating out of a garage.

Still, a number of individuals, teams and organisations are not really delivering to their full potential. Fundamentally it comes down to people who make up the team, society and organisation to deliver to or exceed their individual potential.

If you would like to make a leap in your career and make an impact in your chosen field then becoming a champion of your cause is vital. With a little bit of self-discovery, determination and consistent execution, it is possible to achieve this.

Ordinary Champions will show you exactly how to transform yourself to unleash your full potential, set your own goals and consistently exceed them.

There are a number of blockers to unleashing individual potential and these can be summarised into five elements.

A lack of courage to have a bold vision and the ability to articulate it with confidence. Lack of self-awareness of own strengths and values and ability to harness them. Fears and constraints imposed by the environment which later become self-imposed. Perceived lack of resources to achieve your own goals and a preference for consuming rather than producing.

After a short Introduction chapter, Ordinary Champions will take you through a journey that will help you to discover your passion and identify the cause that you would like to champion and help you create your vision of what you want to achieve in life.

To energise you to go about achieving your vision, you will go through a journey discovering your mountain of value and strengths that you forgot you had. You will learn to harness your strengths and become aware of your weaknesses.

To empower yourself, you will go through a discovery process to identify your fears, constraints and inhibitions and start to eliminate them. You will learn to identify the characteristics of the environment that imposes constraints on you and will start to manage them to your own advantage.

To enable you to achieve your goals, you will learn the importance of acquiring knowledge in your chosen subject area and the power of staying relevant and current. You will discover that the resources that you require to pursue your goals are plentiful and you just need to seek them out.

You will learn to set your own expectations of yourself and regularly achieve or exceed them. This will be achieved by consistently setting and executing your own plans and delivering outcomes that are meaningful to you and those around you. You will learn to identify your own cause and become a champion of it.

Finally, each step of your journey will be supported by real-life examples of people like you achieving amazing successes in their life by following some or all of the above techniques.

After you have gone through the seven steps of the method, the chapter that follows will provide you with a deep insight into the environment within which you operate, providing clarity on why it is this way and what to do about it.

Ordinary Champions will provide you deep insights into your own self, equip you with techniques and motivate you to identify your own cause and successfully champion it professionally and personally.

Based on the feedback from a number of our beta readers, how you read the book will depend on what you want out of it. Some readers read the book and found inspiration to follow their dreams. Some readers diligently went through each of the steps and undertook each of the exercises before they moved on to the next step.

You might want to read the full book once to understand the concept, method and its spirit. Then take multiple follow-on passes through the seven steps of the method and try out the exercises.

Manoj Agarwal

MANOJ AGARWAL

FOREWORD
ELAINE BAKER

Viktor Frankl's best-selling book, "Man's Search For Meaning - The classic tribute to hope from holocaust" is an enduring piece of work. In his book, Dr Frankl observes that it was the hope, dreams and a purpose that kept the prisoners, who were stripped to a naked existence, alive. He quotes Friedrich Nietzsche's words "He who has a *why* to live for can bear with almost any *how*".

We all start with a bigger goal, a lasting purpose. Our purpose gives us courage, energy, and resilience. But along the way, we lose direction and lose faith and end up not realising our full potential. Manoj has created what I believe to be an exceptional piece of work in the form of "Ordinary Champions", which will help you rediscover your purpose, energy, and courage.

I have known Manoj for more than 15 years and have seen him grow from a submissive person constrained by his handicap to a rebel, articulate and successful leader. His own transformation is a testament to the method, quotes, anecdotes and stories presented in his book and I am really glad he decided to finally write it.

Ordinary Champions is all about how ordinary individuals can achieve their full potential. However, as the subchapter "Climbing the Stairs" describes, our role as a leader, coach and mentor can accelerate that achievement. As Manoj's own story shows, it can transform lives and create future leaders.

Unwavering support and faith in your efforts, from

those you hold in high regard, is extremely powerful and helps achieve the unthinkable.

I was lucky in my early years to work for some incredible and pragmatic leaders who were masters in their field, who taught me that there is no limit to ambition if you try hard enough and deliver to your customers.

It is topical to talk about diversity and inclusion but real leaders value all contributions and encourage the whole team to be the best it can be, regardless of background, education or experience. More and more, today, this really makes a difference and ensures the best potential for individuals and businesses.

Often the least experienced in the specific domain has the best idea or concept, which can overturn current thinking or 'group think'. The challenge is getting your voice heard and for the insight to be valued. Finding the way through to achieve your goals requires some deep thinking and a willingness to think differently.

This book provides insights and examples of how focus and tenacity can achieve great things in life and how support can be found from colleagues who have the interests of the team at heart.

It also shows how working towards your goals, consistently and against whatever challenges appear, will triumph in the end.

I hope 'Ordinary Champions' will provide you not only an interesting read but will also rekindle your dreams and give you courage and a sense of purpose.

Elaine Baker
Industry Leader in Systems Engineering

FOREWORD
NORBERT LIECKFELDT

I am usually sceptical of self-help books but I enjoyed Manoj Agarwal's short book. Despite his stammer (or because of it?), he has achieved not only great career success but has also found deep insights along the way.

He asks the reader to find their core – to peel away the layers of unhelpful attitudes and behaviours which we develop over the years, because not to do so might cause problems, might make others dislike us, might be socially risky or unacceptable. This is especially relevant for people who stammer – stammering is associated with a significant social stigma and many people will expend a lot of energy, social capital and avoidance behaviours to hide the fact that they stammer.

Manoj is clearly passionate and manages to convey this passion in simple but insightful and helpful examples. Leadership to him means contributing our own passion to the greater good, not the pursuit of material possessions or status.

The book shares important, small steps to achieving your goals that feel real and achievable. It asks important questions such as "What are the top five reasons that you are not doing what you should be doing?" in exercises following each chapter, and making statements that ought to be obvious but far too often aren't, especially when we are all far too prone to have self-limiting beliefs "You do not require anyone's permission to become an expert."

Not every one of us can become a CEO of a FTSE 100 company but every one of us can follow our passion and do what we are good at, what we enjoy doing and what gives us energy when we are doing it – playing to our strengths, in other words.

I found a lot in here to make me stop and think.

Norbert Lieckfeldt
Chief Executive
British Stammering Association

1 INTRODUCTION

"We are born with the purest of mind and heart, with an abundance of creativity, passion, innocence and playfulness. These fundamental qualities get contaminated as we grow and learn to adapt to the environment around us. The key to unlocking our true potential is to rediscover the purity of our mind and heart."

I believe that every individual has an inherent ability to achieve amazing things in life. At the same time, I also feel that the world around us does not naturally allow our potential to be unleashed to the fullest.

When I meet people, I try and get an opportunity to get behind the scenes and understand their real story. Every time I discover a story behind a face, it is full of surprises, incredible journeys, dreams, hopes, promises, personal achievements, determination and pride. The story that I discover is also full of compromises, constraints, regrets and a deep feeling of unfilled potential.

Once I start to peel the layers of the onion, the hidden core comes alive. At the core, I find passion, core beliefs, innocence, fearlessness, strong values and a deep sense of purpose. The layers hiding this amazing core are self-imposed constraints and fears, low self-value, a burden to meet other's expectations, being pre-judged and a learnt behaviour to conform to the norms of the society, organisation and environment.

As we grow old, the layers become so thick that the core all but disappears and we forget who we really are. We become a slave of the layers hiding our core. We then become part of the environment that helps to create these same layers and contribute to hiding the core of others around us.

This is how a toddler loses the innocence as part of growing up.

FINDING MY INNER CORE

I have had an acute stammer for as long as I can remember. For me, the world was not a very nice place. I dreaded someone asking for my name. The most difficult task for me was to introduce myself. Simple things in life such as buying a train ticket, attending school, playing with other children, attending social functions were actually the most difficult things for me. Most of the people around me, though mostly sympathetic, discounted me. They discounted my potential to achieve simple things in life. I discounted myself.

They pre-judged me even before they knew me. As soon as I stammered, I became beneath them. They were surprised if I accomplished even a small win as if I did not deserve it. They tried to speak on my behalf. They proudly presented my work as if they were doing a favour for me. To hide my stammer, I used some specific support words. They gave me names due to my use of these words. They boxed me into what they thought I was good at.

It was a struggle, every day, to rise above the judgment, hurt, obstacle, fear and challenge of everyday life and continue to move forward creating value in a way that created a sense of fulfilment for me.

To continue with my normal professional and personal life, I needed to discover my core every time I had a setback. This gave me my inner strength to continue the fight. The setbacks were pretty regular, almost every day. That was because the layers were imposed almost every day. Whenever I compromised with the situation, the layers only got thicker and rediscovering the core became harder.

I was fortunate, on two occasions in my life, to come across some great people who put their trust in me. They discovered my core and realised the potential I had. They then helped me to uncover and unleash my full potential. The most notable of them, Elaine Baker, taught me how to be a fighter and a rebel and not accept the things as they are.

With their help, I went through a process of applying a number of techniques to overcome my stammer. The last occasion was in 2004 when I delivered my first ever successful formal presentation to an audience of 30 senior managers from a large UK based utility company. This was the turning point, I had re-discovered my core and I was not going to let it go this time. I have never looked back since then.

The techniques that I developed over the years helped me to have a successful and fulfilling career beyond my own expectations.

HELPING OTHERS TO FIND THEIR INNER CORE

After the experience of my successful presentation, I suddenly found myself trying to catch up with all those lost years. I went out to seek increasingly responsible roles and found myself in leadership positions. With support from Elaine Baker, David Patterson and a few others, there were no fears, constraints or blockers that I could not tackle. There was no job I could not do and no challenge that I could not handle. I was unstoppable.

I became very successful. I also became arrogant, success does that to you sometimes and it is also part of growing up. I did not realise at that time but I was now putting layers on others around me and suppressing their core.

I was again fortunate to encounter Judy Butler (now Judy Holliday) who taught me one of the most important lessons of my career.

My future success no longer depended on how well I did but how well the people working for me and working with me did. It is easy to be really good but very difficult to be great. Judy asked me to go and buy 'Good to Great' by Jim Collins and read it.

This was another turning point for me and I acquired two lifelong habits:

I started to read great books and I still read at least one book every month. It helps me to stay near to my core.

I started to discover the inherent hidden potential in those who I worked with and I started to help them uncover it in the same way as others helped me. I started to become humble. I started to transition from being a manager to a leader.

This was Judy's doing.

What I discovered was an eye-opener. I have a handicap. Yet, I saw so many people around me who are made handicapped without a handicap.

They had an amazing core which was hidden by same layers of self-imposed constraints and fears, low self-value, the burden to meet other's expectations, being pre-judged and a learnt behaviour to conform to the norm of the society, organisation and environment.

Largely, they faced the same challenges, judgement, hurt and fear on a daily basis as I did as a stammerer. They held themselves back and they were not fighting on. They were getting conditioned to conformity.

By this time, I knew how to uncover the core.

I used the same techniques at my work to enable numerous people in my teams to deliver outstanding results both collectively and individually. I became known for my transformative approach to delivering organisational objectives.

People thought that I always delivered results because of my execution, management and technology skills. On the contrary, it was my people transformation skills and it was always those people who were the real heroes who delivered the actual successes. A number of them achieved what they thought was never possible for them. Each of them found their niche and became a champion of it.

The environmental constraints no longer mattered. It was their inner strength that took over.

THE MILLENNIALS CONTEXT

The individual potential is encapsulated inside this amazing core we all have.

As we grow in this world, the core gets hidden inside layers and layers of constraints, fears, conformity, and expectations imposed by those around us. The older we become, the thicker the layers. The thicker the layers, the more difficult to peel back and discover the core. After a certain stage, we become an integral part of the environment and forget that we even have a core.

So, we need to start peeling the layers away before they become too thick and subsume the entire core.

The generation born between 1980 to 1996, the Millennials, holds tremendous promise for our future. Like every generation before them, they dream of a well-lived life, but on their own terms.

This is the most wired generation and socially well connected. They are passionate about the causes that affect the community. They care about the world around them. They have a strong sense of self.

Millennials are our rainmaker. They are the future

pathfinder. They are disrupting the established industries. They are radically changing how business is conducted. They are challenging the established institutions and traditions. They are championing equality and social justice.

They deeply care about the cause they are passionate about. Each one of them has the potential to champion his or her cause and make the world a better place.

By 2020, Millennials will form more than 50% of the world's productive workforce.

They have a stronger core.

They are also unhappy. They have a feeling of getting left behind. They are sad because they think that they are not achieving their full potential. They are tired of always trying to meet the expectations of others.

The world around them does not understand them. It undervalues them. It judges them. It imposes its rules and traditions upon them. It expects them to meet its expectations, not theirs. It imposes an unproductive hierarchy. It imposes stifling bureaucracy. It puts constraints on them. It stops them from achieving their dreams. It kills their hope and it frustrates them.

The layers are trying to hide the core.

We need to help them stay near to their core and show them how to peel back the layers before the layers get too thick. The challenges are the same but the promise is far greater. The techniques that I developed to discover and unleash my own core are equally applicable and probably even more relevant for Millennials.

SUMMARY

Everyone is created equal with equal potential. Everyone learns to crawl. Everyone learns to walk and everyone learns to speak. Some come with special gifts and some come with certain handicaps.

Every one of us has come into this world to fulfil a purpose. From then on our environment dictates who we become.

I believe you can decide who you become. I believe you can outperform your own expectations. I believe you can unleash your true potential. It is entirely down to you, nobody else, to achieve what you are meant to achieve. You owe it to yourself.

The LEAP method of becoming an Ordinary Champion, explained in detail in this book, will help you achieve just that.

Imagine what the world around us would look like if we could unleash the potential of millions of ordinary individuals and help them to feel successful in their own unique way.

The chapters that follow will provide a seven-step guide to leapfrogging in your career. At the end of each step, there is a small exercise for you to do before you move onto the next step.

To get the full benefit from this book, please try and put an honest effort in completing the exercises as you come to the end of each chapter.

By the time you reach the end of this book, you will notice that:

Your perception of your own-self has changed

Your criteria of your success has changed

Your definition of your career has changed

2 SEVEN STEPS TO BECOMING AN ORDINARY CHAMPION

"Being a champion is not about winning, it is about losing but still vigorously supporting and pursuing a greater cause. It is about having a purpose and an extreme devotion to that purpose. It is not about defeating others, it is about outperforming yourself. It is about making a difference."

In his bestselling book, 'Entrepreneur Revolution', Daniel Priestley argues that the next revolution will be led by millions of independent, free-thinking, entrepreneurial people doing what they are passionate about, making a livelihood from it and championing the causes close to their hearts.

I agree with this prediction. About 250 years ago, landowners were the centre of commercial activity and power. During the Industrial Revolution, this power shifted to corporates. Today, some corporates are richer and more powerful than some of the countries in this world.

Slowly but surely, the centre of economic activity has now started to shift to platforms. These platforms will bring together millions of people in the most collaborative economic eco-system. It has started to happen. Look at Amazon, It already allows you, sitting in your bedroom, to be an entrepreneur, seller, an author, a reviewer and a buyer, all at the same time.

So, the rules of the game are changing fast. Technology has provided the right tools. We need to create an environment, to harness these tools and for the individual potential to be unleashed to the full.

This is the right time to step out of the constraints, identify your passions, set your goals, seek resources and create something worthwhile that you can be proud of. Champion the cause that you care about the most. Set your own rules. Set your own expectations.

OUTPERFORMING YOURSELF

We all have a few role models who we worship. We wish to emulate them and to replicate the success they have had in our own life. This has a positive effect on us as we use our role models to draw inspiration, learning and courage.

We also have a tendency and deep desire to meet the expectations of others around us or to prove ourselves in others' eyes. A number of times we want to outperform our peers, friends or colleagues.

You want to feel respected and valued and look for approval and recognition from those around you. You work extremely hard but most of the time the recognition that you crave from those around you does not come in the quantity and form that you expect. You end up getting disappointed, frustrated and de-motivated. Your individual growth stops and you give up trying.

The question is do you really have to do anything to prove yourself to others? No. The only person you need to prove something to is yourself. Set your own goals, tell yourself that "I am going to do it" and go ahead and do it. If you do this, the power of accomplishment is immense. If you don't, well, you will have difficulty in facing your own conscience and that is a powerful force. So you are going to do it.

Find your own mountain and set about climbing it. It is empowering. It is a meaningful accomplishment. You set out to do something that required a significant amount of effort, and then you carried through with it and are now standing on the top. You feel good about this. You should then find the next higher mountain and set about climbing it and carry on with the next and so on until you have nothing to prove to yourself.

During your daily lives, you climb numerous mountains all the time, but these are not your mountains, not your goals and not your ambitions, these are someone else's mountains. So, go climb your own mountain, then the next one and the one after that and continue to feed yourself with the tremendous sense of self-achievement.

Highly accomplished people never retire; they continue to climb a new mountain even if they have achieved everything they ever thought they need to. They have nothing left to prove to anyone but everything to prove to themselves. They do not need to outperform anyone else but themselves.

Bill Gates, at the age of 61, is climbing another mountain:

"Guided by the belief that every life has equal value, the Bill & Melinda Gates Foundation works to help all people lead healthy, productive lives. In developing countries, it focuses on improving people's health and giving them the chance to lift themselves out of hunger and extreme poverty."

So, go and outperform yourself.

FROM ZERO TO HERO IN 90 DAYS

Here is a real-life story of a Millennial who set herself an audacious goal and not only proved everyone else wrong but exceed her own expectations.

Sherry worked hard for her AS levels but when the results came out she was extremely disappointed. In her two favourite subjects, Economics and History, she got a grade 'D', the worst you can get.

During a subsequent meeting with her teacher, she was told that she is not 'A' grade material. She should aim to re-sit all the three papers – Economics-1, Economics-2 and History in about three months' time and work towards getting a respectable 'C' grade.

When I heard this, I was appalled. I am of the belief that everyone has the inherent potential to perform and it is the environment around us that prevents us from unleashing our potential. We have no right to judge others and place a limitation on what they could and could not achieve.

Sherry, clearly suffering from low self-esteem at this point, wanted to jump off a bridge. I offered her the choice of me driving her to the bridge or her letting me coach her for the next 90 days to turn her world around. She agreed to let me coach her. She clearly made the right choice!

During detailed discussions with Sherry, I soon worked out she had deep subject knowledge as she was passionate about both the subjects, but her knowledge was not structured according to the demands and structure of the curriculum.

She knew the answers to most of the questions, but her answers were not structured to maximise the marks in accordance with the prescribed marking scheme. The detail in the answers needed to vary depending on the marks each question carried.

In addition, she was making some common mistakes such as drawing the graphs using pencils. She was not aware that the answer sheets are scanned and delivered electronically to the examiners for marking. Any graphs or illustrations created using pencil would lose clarity during the scanning process and hence she was losing marks.

During classroom interactions, the teacher expected the answers in accordance with what was written in the book rather than what was relevant within the current socio-economic context. The teacher discouraged answers which did not conform to his understanding of the problem irrespective of the fact if the answers were correct or not. This resulted in a loss of self-confidence for Sherry.

In summary, Sherry did not understand how the system worked and despite understanding the subjects, she could not get respectable marks as she did not comply with the rules imposed by the system.

So, we discussed. As she had grade 'D' and the teacher is suggesting to aim for a "respectable grade C", what should she aim for given that there are only 90 days left before the re-sit exams and she will need to work on three exams - so about 30 days for each exam if she did not take any holidays.

Sherry was passionate about both the subjects, she was disappointed by her performance and was devastated by the lack of confidence shown in her by her teacher.

She had a choice, work to meet the expectations of her teacher or set her own expectations of herself and exceed them.

She set her own goal to get, wait for it, 90% marks in all three papers.

To achieve this, Sherry created a highly disciplined plan for the next 90 days. She needed to understand the system and beat it at its own game. At a high level, it included:

> Understanding the structure of the curriculum and focus her studies in accordance with this structure

> Understanding the marking scheme. The same question needs to be answered differently

depending on how many marks it carries. If the question carries one mark, the answer is different to if the question carried eight marks. She needed to really get behind the marking scheme to develop an ability to understand which question carries how many marks and how to answer it so that the examiner has no opportunity to deduct any marks.

The focus needed to shift from how to get maximum marks to how to get no marks deducted. She went for practice, practice and practice on past papers and sample papers until her answers were such that there was no opportunity to deduct any marks.

She needed to listen to the BBC World Service - World Business Report, every day and relate the current world events to the theory of economics and events in the history. Then whenever the teacher asked any question in the class, put your hands up to give the answers for every question. The answer this time needed to answer the question in relation to the curriculum and the book but also related to the current events happening across the world.

The last point above was very important. Sherry was still spending a large part of her day in school and it was important for her to create an environment at school that did not erode her self-confidence.

The BBC World Service trick worked. After only 15 days, Sherry started to put her hand up to any and every question that was asked in the class. She related her answers to the textbook but more so to the context of the current world events. The teacher clearly was not amused but the class liked her answers. She started to be seen as a thought leader on the subject within the class by other students. The teacher stopped harassing Sherry and she really started to look forward to attending the class.

Sherry sat through the re-sit exams and then waited eagerly for the results.

The results came. Sherry got:

Economics-1 - 100%

Economics-2 - 94%

History - 100%

Sherry had outperformed herself and exceeded her own expectations. At this point, she had to answer to no one.

THE LEAP METHOD

I have very different views about the annual exercise of setting team's objectives. My belief was that setting objectives at the beginning of the year will put a constraint on what individuals can achieve. For my teams, we would discuss how far we have come and where we could go if we really put our minds to it. We would discuss the choice of mountains in front of us that we could climb. We would discuss big goals for our department, teams and individuals - big transformative goals. Looking back, almost everyone achieved more at the end of the year than they thought they would at the beginning of the year.

It was important for us to define why we do what we do and everyone worked hard for their own why and the collective why of the team. A number of individuals achieved outstanding success and exceeded their own expectations.

It is not hard to become free from the constraints that the environment around us imposes on us and become successful in identifying and championing our very own cause. Sherry's example above is not the only one. If you look carefully behind the scenes of a number of people around you, a lot of them have achieved outstanding success in their own eyes defying the odds.

Numerous individuals, I have spoken to, who believe that they are not achieving their full potential, agree that there are three main problems that they are facing:

A lack of self-confidence

A low sense of achievement

Unhappiness at being held back by the environment around them

This results in a deep feeling of getting left behind.

There are seven steps that you need to take consistently and repeatedly to become really successful in whatever area you choose:

STEP-1: Identify your passions

STEP-2: Develop a vision and clearly articulate it

STEP-3: Understand your chosen subject, stay current and seek resources

STEP-4: Leverage your strengths and know your weaknesses

STEP-5: Identify your fears and confront them

STEP-6: Identify your constraints and eliminate them

STEP-7: Execute – become a prolific producer

If you embrace the above method, you will:

Achieve a high self-awareness of your own values

Consistently deliver meaningful outcomes

Be respected, recognised and rewarded

This will result in you outperforming yourself and exceeding your own expectations.

In the subsequent chapters, I will explain each of these steps in detail and will support them with real examples of normal people like you and me who have defied the environmental constraints and have made a big positive difference.

MANOJ AGARWAL

3 STEP-1: IDENTIFY YOUR PASSIONS

"There is something that wakes me up in the middle of the night, gets me up in the morning, puts a smile on my face and makes my eyes light up. It is an idea, a problem to be solved, a wrong that needs to be put right together with a burning desire to see it through. It is the thing that I am passionate about."

We spend most of our waking hours at work. Our success at work affects almost all aspects of our life including our happiness, self-confidence and our financial well-being.

Unfortunately, quite a few of us do not invest the required time, thought or energy into planning our career, staying ahead and, most importantly, staying relevant.

With the right amount of focus, strategy, discipline

and execution, it is possible to take a leap in your career. If we can enjoy what we do, we will be successful in what we are trying to do.

Ian Elliott went from being a truck driver to a mail boy, to the CEO and Chairman of Australia's biggest ad agency.

One day, while driving his truck, Ian worked out that his true passion was marketing and advertising and he was in the wrong place driving a truck. It was his passion that took him to the absolute height of the advertising and media industry in Australia and he retired at the age of 48.

Find out what you are passionate about and harness the energy that comes with this passion. If you do something you are passionate about, you will enjoy doing it. If you enjoy doing something, believe me, you will be really good at it. If you are really good at something, people will come to you to do it for them. So, why waste time doing something that you are not really passionate about.

If you are looking to leapfrog your career, you don't necessarily need to change your job. You just need to become really good at it. Find out the aspect of your job that you are really passionate about and do more of it. At your heart, are you a problem solver? A fixer? A people person? An investigator? A top class coordinator? A speaker? A presenter? A salesperson? Or maybe an executor. Working this out is the hardest part.

Most of our working day is spent doing things; checking emails, filling in time sheets, attending meetings, sending and reading minutes, processing transactions on the same computer system, etc. We tend to lose our ability to stop and think. There are very few 'Ah...ha' moments.

Look for those eureka moments when you say to yourself... "Ah...ha, I enjoyed doing that." Stop and think why you enjoyed doing it. Try and recall similar experiences in the past when you got a sense of satisfaction and fulfilment. Then try and work out the patterns.

Look for instances, when you made someone happy, without even trying to. What did you do? You think that you did what you normally do, but you need to get behind that act. That is where your passion lies.

Once you have worked this out, don't try to be someone else. Just being yourself brings the best out in you.

DOING WHAT YOU ARE PASSIONATE ABOUT

Have you ever thought about how people get their dream job? Assuming that you have already worked out what your dream job really is and why - let us try and answer the 'how' question now.

The answer is three words: passion, drive, and determination.

Merriam-Webster defines that passion is an

"Intense, driving, or overmastering feeling or conviction".

You cannot fake it, people can see it in your eyes.

To make it real, let me tell you a little story. The story of Ian Elliott.

Over 30 years in the highly competitive advertising industry, Ian Elliot rose from a mail boy to the CEO and Chairman of Australia's biggest agency, George Patterson. He's a master strategist in brand building and new business acquisition. At just 48 he retired from the advertising industry to focus on his public and private company board responsibilities. He's on the board of a number of top 200 companies in Australia.

Ian was a truck driver and his father was a boilermaker and welder. Truck driving was a job that Ian did but it was not a job that he enjoyed. What he was passionate about was the power of words to influence people and their actions – advertising. One day Ian just packed up and left his truck driver job. He decided to get into advertising and do any job that was available as long as it was in an advertising company.

Over the next three weeks, he visited close to 45 advertising agencies in Sydney looking for any job and nobody would let him in. Ian had nothing to offer in terms of skills or experience and Australia was in a recession. The 46th agency was George Patterson.

George Patterson had advertised for a dispatch boy. Ian managed to meet a lady there who was the Payroll Manager. She soon realised that Ian had no skills or qualifications for the job. Upon further questioning, she came to realise that Ian had such a passion for advertising that he had been walking the streets of Sydney knocking on the doors for last three weeks and had been to 45 agencies so far. Ian had meticulously made notes about every agency he visited, who he met and any other information he learned about the agency.

She was moved by Ian's passion, drive and

determination and she not only shortlisted him for an interview but also coached him on how to pass the interview. Ian got the job as dispatch boy at George Patterson and rest is history.

Personally, I would value true passion, drive, and determination over experience and skills. The former are part of a person's being and cannot be coached or learned.

Skills and experience, on the other hand, can be acquired. If you have the drive and determination, your ability and willingness to learn about the subject you are passionate about increases and therefore acquiring the necessary skills is not really that difficult.

So, how do you find your dream job?

Find out what you are truly passionate about. What makes you happy and what gets your brain cells going into overdrive. Once you have worked this out, pursue it with full determination and drive, and your dream job will find you!

EXERCISE

Try and provide honest answers to the questions below to help you discover your passions:

List out three things that you enjoy doing most.

Try and remember three occasions when you made someone really happy.

If you only have one day to live, what would you spend that day doing?

4 STEP-2: DEVELOP A VISION AND CLEARLY ARTICULATE IT

"You don't have to be a visionary to have a vision. Your vision reflects your desire to move forward. It represents who you are and what you stand for. It inspires you and those around you, whose help you need to make it a reality."

Now that you know what you are passionate about, work out what you want to achieve and where you want to get to. Research the roles that play to your passion and strengths.

Observe the world around you. Research successful people. Know everything there is to know about people you admire. Research some famous people and find out how their vision changed the world. Martin Luther King on 'I have a dream…', President Kennedy's vision on sending a man to the moon, Bill Gate's vision of putting a computer in every home and Steve Job's vision of turning powerful technology into easy to use tools.

Find out what frustrates you. Work out what makes you happy. What are the causes that you care about the most?

If money was no object what three things you would do to support the causes that you care about.

The answers to these questions must come from deep inside you. If your answer is that you want to be the CEO of your company. Fine, but why? If your why is related to the power, money and status you will have, then there are plenty of other ways of acquiring those. But, if your answer is related to the big positive impact that you would like to make on your company's employees, customers, partners and shareholders, this is a cause worth pursuing.

Your current environment and daily life constrain you and your thinking. Go back to your childhood and work out what you really liked. That was the most positively innocent period. You would have played football if you really liked it. You will not play cricket, no matter how much your parents forced you to if you did not enjoy playing cricket.

In your teens and during your college years, you definitely wanted to change the world and had strong views on issues affecting the world around you. You need to rekindle that rebel thinking a little bit.

There are a hundred things that are wrong with the environment that you operate in, with the society, with the politics and with the world in general. But what are you doing about it? What tiny role you could play to make a difference and make it better?

Big leaders have big visions and they have the ability to articulate it with clarity and conviction.

Ordinary people like you and me also have a big vision - we just do not have the courage to talk about it.

Find that courage and tell whoever will listen, what you would really like to do.

Talk about your vision and plan with the passion that it deserves. It will help bring clarity to yourself and to those around you. If you believe in it and talk about it a thousand times, you will bring it to reality. If you demonstrate true belief, passion and drive while talking about it, people will love it and will rally around you to help you achieve it.

Your big vision can easily relate to your current job. You can make a big difference while doing what you are doing currently but doing it with passion and enjoying it as it supports your cause.

Once you have worked it out, your vision will be solving certain problems and making an impact. Those problems may relate to your team, your department, your customer, your organisation, the society or the world. Whatever small impact your vision will make, it will be your impact.

Have a rolling five-year vision and one-year roadmap. Then create a rolling 30-60-90 days plan. Your 30 days plan starts today, not tomorrow.

CLIMBING THE MOUNTAIN

Ever wondered why people climb mountains? Different people have different reasons but one common thread running across them is to obtain a sense of great self-achievement and self-pride. It is to prove to themselves that they can do it, to overcome their own fears, to test their own resilience and endurance and simply to get to know their true self. They don't set out to conquer the mountain, they set out to conquer themselves.

They choose their own mountain, not someone else's. They climb their own mountain, not someone else's. They choose their own role models, like-minded companions and speed. They are not competing with anyone to reach the top faster. They want to enjoy the journey, the life lessons that it brings, the insights it provides and their own sense of successes and failures.

My son, when he was working for a financial services company as an investment banker, had a strong ongoing desire to go climb mountains. He did that and climbed Mt Kilimanjaro and a few others. He then left his corporate job to become a co-founder of a tech start-up to disrupt traditional players. Four years on, he's stopped climbing mountains because he is climbing numerous mountains of his own choosing every day.

I have climbed numerous mountains throughout my life. All of my choosing and to prove something to myself. I had a chronic stammer and in certain situations could not even say my name let alone express my views and Ideas. My mountain was to be able to present a solution for a high-value bid to senior IT leadership of a large utility company in 2004. I have not looked back since then and my stammer has all but disappeared.

Working in a constrained corporate environment does take its toll on your self-esteem. I have approached some of my close friends who share the same values and we decided to climb a mountain. We decided on a big audacious goal that we set out to achieve in our personal time and it resulted in us regaining tremendous energy and sense of self-worth in addition to a number of precious life skills that we learnt.

We always knew what we wanted to achieve and where we wanted to go but did not have a clue how we would get there. It was hard and tough with plenty of tears and joys. The experience of charting a path into the unknown, sharing little successes and failures along the way, discovering both the terrain around us and each other and ourselves, made us realise the inherent potential we had.

To re-energise my team I have often encouraged them to set big goals for themselves and encouraged them to set their sights on the highest peak that they could see and go climb it. The result is a number of high achievers in the team who have had personal and team successes beyond their wildest dreams.

If you are reading this book, I am sure you have always wanted to climb a mountain. What stops you is a fear of failure or the fear of unknown. It is not about success or failure, it is about experience and joy of doing it. You will be a different person making a sincere attempt at it. So, go find your mountain and start climbing it.

VISUALISE THE PRIZE

At the 2004 Summer Olympics at Athens, Sir Matthew Pinsent won his fourth consecutive gold medal.

The British men's coxless four of Steve Williams, James Cracknell, Ed Coode with Pinsent at stroke narrowly saw off the challenge of the World Champion Canadian crew of Cameron Baerg, Thomas Herschmiller, Jake Wetzel and Barney Williams.

It was a dramatic stretch run with the lead literally changing hands with each stroke. (In rowing, the boat will surge depending on where the rowers are in the stroke. Pinsent would later say that he thought they had won because they were in the best part of the stroke when they crossed the line).

Great Britain won with a time of 6:06.98, just 8/100ths of a second faster than the Canadians. Pinsent later wept at the medal ceremony.

I was fortunate to hear Sir Matthew recall this story in person. This was the hardest Olympic medal they had won and by just a few inches. They trained for four years, every day without fail for a final race that would last just 6 minutes and won by a tiny fraction of a second and a few inches.

How do you sustain such extreme training over such a long period of time for such a small win? It was not the small win, this was the ultimate prize. The prize of winning the Olympic Gold. The prize of making the country proud. The prize of pursuing the passion, achieving the vision and fulfilling the dream.

Success is never instant, it is cumulative. It is a long, hard and difficult journey. The trick to completing the journey is being able to visualise the ultimate prize to gain strength and endurance and continue charging ahead with full confidence in yourself.

CLIMBING THE STAIRS

You have a yearning to do something special, climb a mountain and aim for that ultimate prize. The question is what should you aim for? How high could you go? Which path to follow? Once you have reached there, would you have really achieved what you wanted to achieve deep inside you?

Imagine you are standing right at the bottom of a long staircase that is as high as you can see, almost touching the sky. You turn your head up and see hundreds of stairs going up without an end. Your eyes try and focus on the point where you think the top of the stairs is. You decide to aim for that top and start climbing.

Years go by and the climb never ends. There is no top of the stairs. What you think is the top, there is already someone standing there, head turned up, eyes glazing towards the sky and looking for the top of the stairs.

What you need is someone who has already travelled some of the journeys, not necessarily on the same staircase, who can give you some wisdom, tell you that what you think is the top is just a mirage.

You need a mentor or a coach. Someone who sees the passion in your eyes and identifies with your values and cause. Someone who believes in you and sees their success in your success. Someone who can help you identify your passion and clarify your vision. Someone who gives you energy and courage when you are facing defeat or self-doubt.

I have found that regularly reading good quality books also acted as a pathfinder for me. Because people share their journey, thoughts, learning and experiences in the books that they write. Reading gives you a different perspective and helps you to put a different context on the challenges you are facing.

Not everyone is fortunate to have a good mentor or coach. Those who do, leapfrog in their career.

EXERCISE

Try and give honest answers to the questions below to help you clarify your vision:

What frustrates you most in this world?

What are the causes that you care about most?

If money was no object, what single thing you would like to do which will have a lasting positive impact on the world around you?

5 STEP-3: UNDERSTAND YOUR CHOSEN SUBJECT AND STAY CURRENT

"We become irrelevant, not due to old age but because we stop learning. The body has to grow old but the mind can be kept young."

I hope that by following steps one and two, you have some clarity on what you are passionate about, what you want to achieve and where you want to get to. You will also have clarity on the subject area of industry or life that your passion and vision relates to.

You now need to enable yourself to achieve this vision. Steps three and four are all about equipping yourself to start moving ahead with full confidence towards your vision.

Research your chosen subject area. Learn

everything about it. These days, learning and education are free. Reading books is the cheapest and best form of education.

Start writing about and talking to people about your chosen subject.

Geek out on it. Find people who are passionate about the same subject as you, join and build knowledge sharing network. Share the knowledge and ideas. Ask and answer questions.

Learning about the subject that is close to our hearts is a very fulfilling exercise. It increases our sense of achievement. It makes us humble and more confident in our own abilities.

Most importantly, stay current on your subject. The world moves fast and it is all too easy to become irrelevant if you are not constantly updating yourself.

Anyone who stops learning is old, whether at twenty or eighty. Anyone who keeps learning stays young.

Set aside at least one hour every day to read, research and generally geek out on your subject. You might think that you don't have enough time to devote to this on a daily basis. Think again. You have time to watch the TV, time to spend on social networks, time to watch or listen to the news or events on which you have no control.

Try and get up one hour earlier than usual and devote that hour for your self-learning.

Develop a habit of continuous self-learning. Build it as a lifelong passion.

If you are knowledgeable in your subject and stay current, people around you will notice this. You will become known as the expert in your subject area. People will come to you to help them solve their problems. You will be consulted when decisions are made and your expertise is required. You will feel valued, respected and recognised.

You will also develop an ability to help and coach others in your chosen subject.

I have seen some amazing ordinary individuals who have created deep technical expertise in cutting-edge techniques and technologies purely through self-learning, in less than twelve months. They are now an authority in their chosen area of expertise and are called upon by others to help solve complex business problems using these technologies.

You do not need a job title to become an expert in your subject. You do not require anyone's permission to become an expert. The internet and Google have democratised the access to expert knowledge; you just need to find it. It is free.

All you need to do is to learn all the time and keep learning.

BILL GATES - A STORY TO RELATE TO

Some of you may think that Bill Gates is successful because he is super intelligent, he is a techno wizard and he is smart. Think again, for Gates, "Smart is an elusive concept".

In his own words, he attributes his success to his desire to never stop learning. About his team, he says, "There is a certain sharpness, an ability to absorb new facts; to ask an insightful question; to relate two domains that may not seem connected at first." it is this culture of curiosity, the pursuit of knowledge, the quest for answers that Gates tries to inspire in his teams, encouraging them to not only find the answers but to ask the right questions.

Bill & Melinda Gates Foundation is a charitable organisation dedicated to researching new innovations concerning health and education on a global scale. Bill Gates now devotes most his time in the work of this charitable organisation. In this role, he continues to ask questions about the current state of the world and what he can do to both educate others and help relieve the problems.

"Is the rich world aware of how four billion of the six billion live? If we were aware, we would want to help out, we'd want to get involved." - Bill Gates

According to Bill Gates, no matter what you spend your time doing in life, you should never stop asking questions, never stop learning. Whether you're an entrepreneur, a doctor or a software developer, it is only by increasing your understanding of the world around you that you will be able to have a significant impact.

This is why Gates can still exclaim today, "I'm excited by the possibilities." If you never stop learning, you will never stop seeing the possibilities.

EXERCISE

Try and give honest answers to the questions below to help you understand your subject and develop a lifelong learning habit:

> What subject would you like to become an expert in? Try and be specific. For example, if your answer is food, what type of food? Organic food, healthy foods, baby food, reducing food wastage etc.
>
> What three things you will stop doing to find one hour a day for your self-learning?
>
> Who are the three people you know of, who may have a common interest in your subject?

6 STEP-4: LEVERAGE YOUR STRENGTHS AND KNOW YOUR WEAKNESSES

"Enduring success comes by developing the strength of your will and toughness of your mind. To be mentally tough, you must tolerate the intolerable and you must suffer through the insufferable by leveraging your strengths and overpower your weakness and your desire to give up."

Steps one and two will have helped you gain some clarity on what you are passionate about, what you want to achieve and where you want to get to. As we discussed, steps three and four are all about equipping yourself to start moving ahead with full confidence towards your vision.

Step three talked about gaining a deeper understanding of your chosen subject area and developing a lifelong learning habit.

Your passion is a cause that is close to your heart. Your strengths are your skills, values, beliefs and your traits that make you successful. It's important to identify what your strengths are.

Our strengths consist of skills, behaviours and values. Skills can be acquired. Behaviours and beliefs form over a longer period of time and are based on life experiences.

We all too easily forget what we are good at and only see our weaknesses. To identify your strengths, a good idea is to ask someone you trust. Other people see our strengths more clearly than we do.

You will be amazed to discover the strengths and skills that you have that you cannot see. Some are just natural to you, so you don't consider them as your strengths.   Some are unrecognised as you are too modest to admit those as your strengths. You think this is your job. Some have been suppressed by the people around you as these are too threatening to them. Some have become hidden due to the passage of time and normal daily routine of life.   Some strengths only surface within a specific context, such as a crisis or a social occasion.

We, humans, have numerous hidden strengths, tremendous potential and are capable of achieving far more than we actually do.

Try and watch the last twenty years of your life as a happy movie recalling all of your successful moments. Try and work out what made you successful during each of those moments. These are your strengths. Make a list of every strength that you identify however small and trivial. If you do justice to this task and try not to be too modest, your list would have anywhere between

40 to 60 items. Try and identify patterns or themes from this list and you are then looking at between seven to eleven core strengths.

My belief is that every individual has an inherent ability to deliver an outstanding result. So, every individual can arrive at this list of their core strengths. You will not find a single individual who does not have a number of core strengths.

Once you identify your strengths, you should leverage them, multiply their effectiveness and embrace them. Acknowledge them to yourself. 'I am really good at...' It will give your self-confidence a boost. It will provide you with the clarity of thought and purpose. It will bring positivity to your actions.

Do more of the things that play to your strengths. Let your core strengths shine in everything you do. Over a period of time, your behaviours will become more mature, your beliefs and values will become stronger and your skills will become sharper.

Do more of what you are good at. If you are good at writing but not good at public speaking, start writing even more. Start writing now.

As far as your weaknesses are concerned, it is important for you to know them. You will be tempted to, but do not hide them and do not let them constrain you. Do not waste time in fixing them or overcoming your weaknesses unless these are skill-based weaknesses. Instead, spend that time in harnessing your strengths.

They are not your weaknesses, they are just part of who you are and you must have something else to more than compensate for those weaknesses. Some of your weaknesses could be your strengths depending on the context.

Some characteristics that you consider as a weakness can actually be a strength, you just don't realise it. A little child always tells you what she really thinks. As we grow, we adapt to our environment and expectations of others of us. We start to tailor what we say and hide or bend the truth. Which one is a weakness and which one is a strength is very contextual. So, be very careful and diligent in identifying your weaknesses and trying to fix them. You might lose your core strengths in that process. Your strengths are what made you who you are.

To identify your weaknesses, try and watch the last twenty years of your life as a movie recalling all of your moments, where the outcome was not as you expected. After the event, looking back, you think you could have done better than that. Try and work out what made you unsuccessful during each of those moments. Make a list of every shortcoming or mistake that you identify however small and trivial.

If you do justice to this task and try to be honest with yourself, your list would have anywhere between 40 to 60 items. Try and identify patterns or themes from this list and you are then looking at between ten to fifteen core weaknesses or shortcomings. A slightly higher number than strengths, this is human nature for you!

Look at this list and eliminate the ones where the shortcomings are actually a strength based on a deeply held belief or value. If the weaknesses are due to certain values that you hold strongly, trying to fix these will go against your deeply held beliefs and values. So, remove these from the list.

If some weaknesses are due to the lack of skills in an area that you are passionate about, you should create a plan to address these. The previous step about knowing your subject and lifelong learning will help here.

If your weaknesses are due to your behavioural traits, identify and analyse each of these and work out which ones go against achieving your passion and vision. Try and do something about these. Compared to skills, it is much more difficult to change behaviours and you might need some help from a close friend or a mentor.

You should now have a high degree of self-awareness about your own ability to deliver the vision that you created. You will also develop a mature sense of knowing yourself. You will feel more confident when you are dealing with situations as you know what tools (strengths) you have at your disposal and what risks (weaknesses) you need to watch out for.

WATCH THE MOVIE

All of us sit on a mountain of value, we have our own very unique moments of personal success that we are really proud of. Our achievements and successes are our own.

For some of us, a simple task of being able to get up in the morning and go about our daily lives is a success. For someone in a war-torn region being able to survive each passing day is a success. For some, being able to eat, sleep and live is a success. Buying the first house, getting an education despite overwhelming odds, giving a successful presentation, etc. all are examples of successes and moments of personal glory, the value of which is unique to individuals.

The challenges of daily life mean that we tend to forget our own little achievements and the inherent qualities that we have that resulted in those achievements. We can't see the mountain of value we are standing on. Even the people close to us perhaps can't see it as they probably are too close.

You have your own mountain of value that you are standing on and you'll discover it when a stranger happens to hear your story and tells you how well you have done. That is because they can see the mountain that you are standing on.

We go through the ups and downs of the life and sometimes feel defeated by the challenges facing us or confused by the options in front of us or depressed that we are not going anywhere.

If you are going through this phase, it is time to discover your true self, your passion, your motivations, your drivers and your inherent values. The values that created that mountain out of your tiny successes through your life. There is a simple trick to discovering these gems.

You should go into a quiet room, draw the curtains, sit in a corner and watch your own movie as a bystander. The movie where you are the main character and the story starts as far back as you can remember. The movie of your life story so far. The challenges you faced and how you overcame or sidestepped those to move forward. How you applied your wits, your charm, your skills, your perseverance and your values. The long-term relationships you forged and the tactical alliances you entered into.

When faced with choices, what decisions did you make and more importantly why did you make those decisions and who helped you. Which decisions did you regret and why? What value, joy and happiness that you brought to others? The path you travelled, the people you met, and those small number of people who influenced you and made you who you are today.

Watch how far you have come, the great distance you have travelled and the numerous personal mountains you have climbed. Watch your own movie, discover yourself, and discover your inherent values that made you who you are today. Feel elated and much wiser and now move ahead with full clarity and confidence.

YOUR MIND, BODY AND YOU

Have you ever noticed that there are three of you? Your mind, your body and you (your conscience). These three forces are constantly in play with each other trying to find the equilibrium. You do things or don't do them depending on who is winning and you do amazing things when you achieve equilibrium between you, your mind and body.

When you want to get up early in the morning, you know you need to get up but when the alarm goes off your body tells you to just lie down a little bit longer so you hit the snooze button, after a few more snoozes, you suddenly look at the clock and you know that you really need to get up otherwise you will miss the train. That is your mind telling your body to jump off the bed pretty quick.

Most successful athletes, war heroes, business

people show a very high degree of self-discipline. This is a sign of them winning over their mind and body. They go through the process of training themselves to have equilibrium over both their mind and body.

Sir Matthew Pinsent and his team won the Rowing Gold Medal in the Athens summer Olympics 2004 by beating Canadian team by just a few inches. They trained for four years to win and towards the end of the race, the only part of the body that was functioning was the arms and the legs - everything else was virtually shut down. They had trained their minds to divert all resources that the body had to offer to their arms and legs.

Even ordinary people like you and I can achieve this equilibrium by training our minds and body. If you can do it, the results and the self-satisfaction that comes with it is amazing.

One of my close friends asked for my help to help his son. The young boy, who had a brilliant academic performance during his pre-university years, had suddenly lost all hope soon after joining a medical college.

He was consistently underachieving, failing his exams and thus having to repeat the year with younger students. The trauma that followed and the typical social stigma in a campus-based environment meant that he had lost all his self-esteem.

Despite being a person with high intelligence, he lost his ability to analyse, retain and reproduce information even after studying for 8-10 hours a day. He started to crawl more and more into his shell, stopped confiding in anyone and spent hours in a room reading the textbooks, preparing for exams without any success.

His eyes were reading the book but his mind was lost

somewhere else, recreating various events, trying to answer the numerous questions as to how he got here and what a high achiever he used to be. The result was that no information was being retained in the brain. At the end of the day, when he could not recall any of the information he had read through, another cycle of defeat would set in with all the resultant impact on self-confidence and self-esteem.

He will wake up in the morning and continue to lie in bed for hours as there was no desire to get up and there was nothing to look forward to. He did not want to face another day full of defeat.

After an initial conversation and after building some trust, we agreed on a set of smaller wins and a number of steps that will bring him back from this unfortunate state. None of these steps related to his study or books or exams as those were not relevant. They all aimed at building his confidence in his own abilities a little bit at a time.

A number of these were geared towards helping him to find a healthy equilibrium between his mind, body and himself.

First, the mind needed to be cleared of all the negative and depressing thoughts. I discovered that a few years back he used to love to run at the stadium nearby. So, why don't we try that?

If you run at a comfortable pace or just walk briskly, the body acquires an amazing rhythm and after a certain time, you notice your head getting cleared of all sorts of stuff while it concentrates solely on supporting your body to maintain the rhythm.

Soldiers march for hours on the rhythm of the infantry drum. Both mind and body are focusing on working to the rhythm.

If you persevere and still continue walking or running, at one point in time the mind would divert all the resources across the body including itself to supporting your legs as it goes into the survival mode.

At the end of it when you stop, you'll probably be tired but you have a relaxed, clear and focused mind.

It was easier said than done for the young boy as getting up out of bed in the morning was in itself a challenge. He needed something to look forward to in order to get up. Perhaps the joy of running, but he was not there yet.

We agreed that we will speak every day to see how he is progressing with his run.

The first day, we discovered that he did not go for the walk. He lay in bed for hours in his usual depression and then went about his daily routine of reading the textbooks the whole day but not really learning anything.

It was time for some simple things. We agreed that nothing can be achieved unless he gains his self-confidence and self-esteem. In order to do that, he needs to set very small simple goals for himself in the things that he used to love doing and achieve these simple goals.

He had to prove to nobody but himself that he can run for 15 minutes early in the morning and enjoy the fresh air, the feeling of being free, the feeling of being himself and the feeling of achieving this simple goal. Academic success or study was off the table. It is not important at the moment. At this point in time, nothing else matters.

We noticed that when we talked about all these good things he felt energised but as soon as he went back into his environment the depression set in. The environment in which he was living enforced certain expectations on him and he was under pressure to work to meet those expectations and do what others expected him to do not what he wanted or enjoyed doing. The environment and whatever came with it took over his emotions, his mind and his thinking.

So, we agreed that the only thing that mattered was to get up in the morning, jump out of bed and go running.

It took just a few more days for that first crucial step to be taken. But soon enough he was up in the morning and getting outside and started to run.

Initially, it lasted a little more than 15 minutes. But we agreed to gradually increase the running time. The trick we applied was to set the timer in his phone to 15 minutes, start running and stop as soon as the timer goes off.

After a week, his mind and body got trained to continue to run until the timer went off. Then, one day the timer was increased by another 5 minutes and he continued to run until the timer went off.

Using this technique of gradually increasing the time, he eventually was running 4 laps of the stadium. What resulted from this small achievement was a feeling of absolute fulfilment, high self-confidence and even higher self-esteem. Everything else then followed this little success.

I worked with another friend who was very successful in his professional field but who lived a very unhealthy lifestyle – he never went to a gym and never did any exercise. He was overweight and, eventually, soon after he turned 45, he was diagnosed with hypertension, was signed off from work for three weeks and was asked to take rest and medication to recover.

At this point, he really needed some help, not medical help but courage and encouragement to sort himself out. His body was not coping, his mind was depressed and he had not known anything except work throughout all his working life.

He needed to achieve something that he never thought he would achieve, that was to eventually exercise in the gym for 1 hour a day and walk six miles a day. This was his big audacious goal to outperform his inhibitions and fear and get his life back on track. And he had 21 days to achieve it, as this is how long he was signed off from work. This needed to be supported by a complete change of diet, including more healthy options and proteins.

The mind and body both needed to be retrained. He needed to find an equilibrium between his mind, body and himself so that each is supporting others and working in tandem to save him.

We worked out a walking circuit near the home which was about one mile. Day one was a slow walk for a mile in the morning and another in the evening so a total of two miles.

Day two he did two circuits in the morning and one in the evening, about three miles. Slowly increasing the time, he was eventually doing three circuits in the morning and three in the evening with a total of six miles walk a day and at this point, he was enjoying the walking, the freshness of mind, clarity of thought and increased self-confidence. The change in diet was helping too, and he felt better in general.

We now needed to conquer the fear of exercising in the gym. We applied the same trick and he started with five minutes each on a treadmill, a bike and a rowing machine. The body that had never done any exercise could not cope with more than that. The single goal was to do five minutes, which is not much but it allowed the mind to get focused on it and the body duly cooperated.

After about three days of five minutes on each, we were now ready to increase the time in small increments to stretch the body and the mind. It happened and by the end of day ten, he was comfortable in doing 20 minutes each on the treadmill, bike and the rowing machine, a total of 60 minutes of continuous exercise.

The achievement was self-fulfilling and in a further five days, he was doing 30 minutes each on the treadmill, the bike and the rowing machine in addition to walking six miles a day. The transformation was complete; the equilibrium was achieved between his mind, body and his self.

With a little discipline, if you really want to do something, it is not difficult to train your body and mind. So, try the following exercise.

Choose a time most comfortable for you to get up in the morning.

Set the alarm for this time and get up. Don't use the snooze button, just get up. Actually jump out of the bed as soon as you hear the alarm

After a few days, once you are regularly getting up as soon as the alarm goes off, set the alarm for 5 minutes earlier. But don't tell yourself!

The next day, you will see you will get up 5 minutes early more easily.

Keep on reducing alarm time by 5 minutes at regular intervals and very soon you will be getting up one hour earlier without any problems.

You can try the same technique in many other similar situations.

EXERCISE

This one should not be a surprise. I would recommend that you try and spend some quality time to honestly reflect on the below:

> List 50 of your strengths, however small and trivial. Then find out common themes across this list. List top seven strengths.

> List 50 of your weaknesses, however small and trivial. Then find out common themes across this list. List top seven weaknesses.

> List three things that you will do more of and three things that you will do less of to leverage your strengths and manage your weaknesses.

7 STEP-5: IDENTIFY YOUR FEARS AND CONFRONT THEM

"Our fears are like ghosts, they live forever in the corner of our mind, a figment of our own imagination. But when we gather our inner courage and confront them in the face, they disappear "

You have now gone through steps one to four. You have identified what you are passionate about. You have a clear view of what you want to achieve and where you want to go. You have created the key enablers in terms of understanding your subject and staying current, leveraging your strengths and managing your weaknesses.

You now need to empower yourself. Steps five and six are all about self-empowerment. This means identifying and removing the powerful blockers from your path to success.

Your fears are what stop you from being successful. You know what you are passionate about. You know what you are good at. You know where you want to get to. You also know what you need to do in order to get there. You are still not doing it. What is stopping you? It is your fears.

Your fears are self-imposed. You should try to become the child you once were. When you were a child, you had no fear. You would try anything and everything because you had no fear. You would try to walk. You would fall down. You would get up and try to walk again. You would keep on trying and eventually, you would learn to walk. We all do eventually. Where was the fear of falling?

We collect fears as we grow up. Fear of failure, fear of getting found out, fear of what people will think, fear of embarrassment and fear of not meeting other people's expectation of us.

In order to move forward and achieve our true potential, we need to confront and conquer our fears. It is not easy, it is very hard. It takes determination and a childlike courage.

Let us try and identify the fears and do something about them.

Work out what you should really be doing but are not doing. Be honest about it. Make a list of all these items, no matter how small or trivial. Now go through this list and remove the items that you can easily do and will start doing from tomorrow if you can find the time. The remaining items in the list are the items that you know you should be doing but something stops you from doing it. Now list down what stops you from doing these items. This is your list of fears. Let us discuss the three likely candidates you will find in this list.

FEAR OF FAILURE

You are not doing certain things because you are afraid that you will fail. It stops you from moving towards your goal. Well, you will not know until you try. The trick to tackle this is to take small steps. Test and learn. How did you learn to walk? How did you learn to ride a bike?

Shift your objective from achieving a goal to gaining a new experience and going through a journey. Every time you fail in taking small steps, you learn something. You apply this learning and then take the next step. Focus on the journey rather than the goal. Think of climbing a mountain. You climb it for the ultimate pleasure of reaching to the top. But the most fulfilling part is the journey through uncharted paths and unknown obstacles. Take pleasure in experiencing this journey.

Failure is what it is all about. Failure is part of the journey to success. We learn by failing.

FEAR OF GETTING FOUND OUT

You know you have a weakness or a handicap. There is nothing you can do about it. You avoid doing certain things or situations which will expose your weakness. You try and hide or mask the symptoms. As you are worried about getting found out, if you are exposed to these situations, your handicap or weakness becomes even more prominent.

This generates more self-consciousness. Every time you try and hide even more, it becomes worse. This is a self-fulfilling cycle. In my experience, the way to overcome this fear is to openly accept your weakness or handicap. Do not try and hide it. This is part of you. This is what makes you who you are.

FEAR OF EMBARRASSMENT

You are worried about what others will think of you. We do a lot of things and don't do a lot of things to make sure we fit in. We try to meet other people's expectation of us.

Fear of embarrassment can actually be quite damaging. It will tend to impact your confidence. It will discourage you from taking the necessary steps that will help you take advantage of opportunities and get ahead in this world, and it will prevent you from attempting new things.

Stop doing or not doing things due to this reason. Yes, you need to live and behave by the accepted norms of society but as long as you hold strong values and your actions are driven by your deep desire to do the right thing, you should do what you believe to be right.

You do not need to prove yourself to anyone except you. You do not need to outperform anyone; you need to outperform your own expectations of you.

In order to overcome your fears, it might help to go back to your passions and be clear on your why. Why you do what you do. What is the big purpose behind it? How your vision is focused on larger goals. How achievement of those goals will make a positive impact on you and those around you. Remember your strengths. Recall your successes and feel proud of them. This will give you inner confidence to take the steps that you need to take in order for you to move forward.

If you are fearful of something, do more of it. Keep on doing it till it is no longer a fear. As you conquer your fears you will see your effectiveness go through the roof. As Dale Carnegie has said:

"Inaction breeds doubt and fear. Action breeds confidence and courage. If you want to conquer fear, do not sit home and think about it. Go out and get busy."

This is the start of your leapfrog

CONQUERING THE FEARS

Our fears hold us back. We are not able to be our true self due to these fears and are not able to achieve our full potential.

Our success depends on our confidence (in addition to our abilities) and our confidence gets depleted by our own fears. Our fears create self-doubt in our mind and our self-doubt damages our confidence. The more we know, the more we become cautious and fearful of things going wrong.

I had a chronic stammer since my childhood as far back as I can remember. It was a self-fulfilling cycle. If I stammer once, my mind was fearful of stammering every time I tried to speak. The more I stammered, the more the fear of stammering built up, which led to more stammering. The cycle would reach its peak and days will go by without me speaking a single word. Over time, I naturally started to speak and then the cycle will start from the first time I stammer.

I dreaded people asking my name.

I did not want people to know that I stammered, so I avoided situations where I need to speak such as in the class or trying to buy a ticket etc. at the counters. I felt less of a human being or beneath everyone else if I stammered in a group situation. So, I would avoid the group situations.

Speaking in front of authority figures, new people and in group situations were a real challenge for me.

To build up my confidence again, I practised speaking on my own in front of the mirror but most of the time I would still stammer.

Life went on and I mainly confined myself to a very small circle of people, my family, my close friends and my teachers, who already knew I stammered so I had no fear of being found out. As a result, I liked being on my own and did very well academically.

I developed a passion for listening to music; there were certain songs that I enjoyed very much. Listening to these songs took me away from this world and I used to forget all my sorrows and fears.

One of the very strange observations was that I did not stammer when I sang a song I liked. That was because while singing those songs my mind was dormant whilst I enjoyed the song. There was no fear.

During the second year of my engineering degree, I was introduced, by one of my professors Dr Krishna

Kant, to the Director of local Institute of Psychology, a renowned Professor in this field. He used to run group therapy sessions for people who suffered from stuttering. He had developed his own techniques and the full course consisted of 8-10 group sessions over two months with a group of about 10 participants. I enrolled myself into the course and was amazed to find out how many people quietly suffered from the same problem.

The underlying technique was to help us gradually conquer the fear of getting found out that we stammered and get us to a position where we could proudly announce to the world that we stammer. Because once everyone knows that we stammer there was no fear of getting found out and we can be free to speak.

The first session was introductions from each of the participants and we spent the whole two hours introducing ourselves. It takes a long time for a room full of stammerers to introduce themselves to each other.

We started the next session with singing! Each of us would sing a poem specially written by the Professor where stammering was inbuilt within each of the lines. So, we would voluntarily stammer and sing with full-blown stammering mixed with the singing. This was a really funny sight at times. A room full of boys and girls all singing and stammering voluntarily and sometimes involuntarily at the same time!

It took us probably three sessions to master this art of singing with stammering in front of each other without inhibitions and fear but with fun and joy.

We were told that the next session will also be a singing session but with a surprise twist. The twist was that everyone's family was invited to attend. I lived in a hostel so a couple of my teachers and friends came to see us perform.

What came next was beyond belief. We all sang all the poems in full tune and glory with a lot of voluntary stammering sprinkled all over the place in front of our family and friends. We had turned our inherent fears into comedy and fun! There was no longer a shame in stammering in front of our family and friends and other people's family and friends who were present in that room. We all went home really happy and light in our hearts and minds.

We were told that the next two sessions were also singing sessions but will be outdoor and with another twist. So, in a way, we were being prepared to face unknown situations but with support from the group and our practice sessions.

For the next session, we reached the local town square and a real surprise awaited us. The professor had brought a portable loudspeaker with him.

To our astonishment, we were now asked to sing our poems, with full-blown stammering thrown in, on the loudspeaker in the middle of the square in front of the gathered crowd. Some people in the crowd were amused and loved what we were doing but some started to make fun of us. We were encouraged by the professor to join in the fun and not develop fear from the reactions.

When a sizeable crowd was gathered, some of us continued to sing and others, helped by the professor, started to talk to small groups of people and explain our stammering and what we were trying to do, all the time stammering off course but without the fear of being found out.

We repeated the same show at different locations for two days and the experience for us was out of this world. Never before we had so publicly acknowledged our stammering problem, made such a great fun of it and joined other people, complete strangers in sharing this surreal experience with us.

So, the singing was conquered, fear of being found out or being made fun of was conquered. Standing in front of complete strangers and continue to stammer was no longer a humiliating experience.

We now needed to find our true voice without scripted poems. We needed to express ourselves in our own words with our own thoughts, with the confidence that a normal person exhibits while speaking normally. We were a bit far away from being in that position.

For next set of sessions, our professor found a couple of places outdoors with a natural feature that could act as a platform to speak from, almost like a mini stage but much higher. The places were more or less secluded and away from the main road so that we could practice in private without being intimidated by visitors.

This time, to our surprise, each of us, one by one, was asked to go on the platform and shout as loud as we could about anything we fancied. That was a strange experience to start with but a very powerful therapy.

It was almost as if we were shouting and throwing away with full force all our inhibitions, insecurities, hatred and fears. We shouted without regard to any boundaries or anyone else. We did not care what the world thought of us. We threw out all the negativity that was ingrained inside us. And we felt free.

Suddenly after all this shouting on a raised platform in front of the rest of the group, we started to speak naturally and normally. The fear had vanished and we did not notice it, it was normal again.

For the next session, we assembled at the same place with the raised platform and went through the ritual of shouting to let go of our inhibitions and fear for first half an hour.

After this, we were asked to go on the platform one by one and give a speech on a topic of our choice while rest of us acted as audiences. The first sentence had to be a very clear acknowledgement by the speaker to the audience that he/she stammers. Then we would speak calmly for 15 minutes on a topic that was close to our hearts.

Well, I guess this was the moment a number of us were waiting for. We all spoke and very rarely any of us stammered. It was magic. The fear had finally been conquered.

We all experienced an amazing feeling of liberation but deep inside us, we were still fearful about how we would perform in an uncontrolled environment.

I was the only student from the Engineering College and the professor was really proud of the recovery I had made. Our main lecture theatre could accommodate almost 100 people.

To provide something that is close to an uncontrolled environment, we came up with an idea to host our closing session in the main lecture theatre of the Engineering College and I volunteered to invite at least 150 people hoping that at least 100 will turn up.

I now had a big responsibility on my shoulders to go and individually meet as many faculty members and Engineering students as possible. I would then explain to them that I stammer and what we were trying to do and invite them to the event. To help me out, the group raised some money and arranged for light snacks, hoping the free food would help attract students to our event.

I reached out and spoke individually to almost 30 faculty members and 120 students over a two-week period. I was on a mission after my new found freedom and it felt really good. To my astonishment, after hearing what we were trying to do, everybody extended support, it is almost as if they wanted us to be really successful in what we were trying to achieve.

This incredibly positive experience increased my self-confidence to astonishing levels and I was literally flying, going through so many positive emotions that I had never before experienced in my life.

On the day of the event, we were all a little bit nervous as only a handful of people had arrived and it was nearly time to start. We decided to wait for more people to arrive and started to engage in one to one conversations to make ourselves and others feel comfortable whilst we waited for more people to arrive.

Then something happened and within 15 minutes almost everyone I had spoken to had arrived, plus a few more. We were oversubscribed!

Rather than feeling intimidated by such a large number of people packed into every corner of the lecture theatre, we were beaming with joy. The reason was that every single person in that hall was there to hear our story and wanted us to be successful. You could see that on their faces.

So, now we were in an uncontrolled, semi-formal environment in front of close to 150 strangers. We really needed to perform successfully in this environment to cement and bind the confidence that we had gained over the last two months and make this recovery a lasting recovery.

We felt elated, responsible, humble, fortunate and grateful to the Professor, knowing that he had equipped us with all the tools, training, techniques and tips that we could possibly need to give our best performance that day.

We had close to 150 people sitting in front of us who were willing to give their personal time to help us be successful. We felt a strong sense of responsibility to not let any of them down. We had no choice but to finally and forever conquer our fears that day.

After a short introduction by the professor, we all went to the podium, did our trademark singing with a voluntary stammer, in the groups and individually. The reaction from the audience started with bemusement and turned into fun and appreciation, we had never heard so much applause from so many people before.

We did a little round of voluntary shouting to demonstrate technique and emotions and give ourselves a little bit of extra help.

Then we all gave our favourite speeches as we had on those raised platforms. Round after round of applause followed, we all did great. We expressed ourselves fully probably the first time in our lives in front of strangers and we were ourselves. You could see that the people in front of us were happy for us and shared our joy and emotions.

The fear of the stammer was well and truly buried that day. It had been conquered.

After that day, we all went our separate ways. The stammer had been managed but not cured. The fear could come back any time given the wrong environment and conditions. So, I had to continue to set myself challenging goals to keep on top of the fear.

I was academically brilliant and one of the faculties would let me teach his class so I would continue to get practice. I became very good at teaching.

I applied for a commission in the Indian Navy Technical Corps as I had heard that the selection process is very tough with numerous interviews, group discussions and obstacle tests. It was spread over 15 days and we had to stay on an Army campus during that period.

This was a perfect opportunity in an unfamiliar environment to test myself out and for me to practice my techniques and continue to bury the fear of stammering. I went through the selection process and was among the 15 selected for the commission out of 257 participants.

At this point, I had conquered my fear of stammering and had a very successful professional career for the next 13 years or so.

If you have read this far you must have related the story to some of your deep-rooted fears that are obstructing your path to happiness and achieving your full potential.

Human life is precious, the more you achieve your true potential the more you can help those around you achieve their full potential.

So, make an impact, conquer your fears. You owe it to yourself and to those around you.

EXERCISE

In order to do this exercise, you might have to do a little bit of soul searching to find your own inhibitions.
Try and work out honest answers to the following questions:

> What are the top five things, most important for your success, that you are not doing?

> What are the top five reasons that you are not doing what you should be doing?

> What is that one handicap or weakness that you have which gives rise to your fear of getting found out?

8 STEP-6: IDENTIFY YOUR CONSTRAINTS AND ELIMINATE THEM

"The human mind knows no boundaries and human spirit cannot be imprisoned. There are no real barriers to our progress except the ones that we erect for ourselves and for those around us. So, if you want to move forward, crush those barriers."

You have now gone through steps one to five. Steps one and two were about working out who you really are, what you want to achieve and where you want to go. You have created the key enablers in terms of understanding your subject and staying current, leveraging your strengths and managing your weaknesses.

You now need to empower yourself. Steps five and six are all about self-empowerment. This means identifying and removing the powerful blockers from your path to success. In step five, we talked about our fears and how to confront them in order to move forward.

Your fears are self-imposed and your constraints are imposed by others around you. Eventually, they also become self-imposed constraints as you forget who you truly are and your deep strengths become dormant.

Run a mile away from people who put you in a box. Avoid situations that impose such constraints on you that you cannot be yourself.

Constraints are also caused by an ingrained belief system. The belief system has been imposed by the environment around you over a period of time. High-performing environments have highly enabling and optimistic belief systems. Low-performing environments have suppressive and pessimistic belief systems. The environment around you dictates your belief system and in turn, dictates your performance.

Ask yourself what is holding you back in order to identify your constraints and your self-imposed limits. Constraints could be the assumptions that you are making. Such as – you need a university degree to have a good career. Another limiting belief could be that your current environment is holding you back from personality development. Work out if that is really true. Is there someone working in the same environment who has managed to develop himself or herself well?

Seek out people who enable and empower you. Seek out teams, projects, companies and eco-systems that are progressive, optimistic and provide you empowerment and freedom to operate.

Identify your current constraints and eliminate them one by one. Work out what is stopping you from doing what you should really be doing. Why is it stopping you? What assumptions are you making and are these assumptions still true? Do the opposite of what your constraint is forcing you to do and eliminate it. Become a rebel if you have to.

A long time ago, one of my line managers told me that I wasn't a management material. I was boxed into being a worker. I lived with that constraint for years. One day I decided to eliminate it and went to the same line manager to declare that I will find a management role and become the best manager around. That is exactly what I did and I have never looked back. David Patterson gave me my first break by trusting me with managing the multi-million pound account for one of the largest utility companies in the UK.

About 20 years ago, I was denied a career progression opportunity because my manager thought I was not good at selling. To break this constraint and to prove him wrong, I got hold of a list of 100 companies and set about cold calling them. After making about 300 calls I closed three deals. The deals were small but the boost to my self-esteem was very big.

Our constraints or self-limiting beliefs only exist in our minds. Our environment conditions us into thinking that there are boundaries and ceilings that exist and cannot be crossed.

Take the analogy of 'breaking a horse'. A horse is stronger than the man. The man conditions the horse at the very beginning into believing that he is stronger than the horse. Once the horse is broken into believing that man is the master, the man rides the horse and horse never thinks of breaking this self-imposed limit.

Once you start to identify and eliminate your constraints, you are really leapfrogging.

DISCOVER YOUR INNOCENCE

Childhood innocence is a very powerful force. Children act, behave and speak without any constraints and we love them for it. Children demonstrate a certain passion in everything they do. We then slowly grow up and that innocence and passion get buried somewhere deep inside us.

We become increasingly aware of the environment around us and are tuned to behave and act in a certain manner. What is the acceptable way of sitting at a dinner table, acceptable ways of engaging with people in social gatherings, etc? We are constantly reminded of the unwritten rules that should govern our behaviour.

It gets even worse when we get our first job. We go through a thorough induction process and are expected to follow even more rules. Our creativity and passion start to take a back seat and we become a prisoner to these constraints that the environment has imposed on us. We lose our inner voice and we start to mask our innocence to conform to the environment around us.

We become fearful of expressing our emotions and passions due to the self-imposed constraints.

I overcame my acute stammer in Engineering College because I felt free to express myself, my emotions and passions without fear or constraints.

Sometime during 1999, my company was acquired by a big IT Services corporate. It was a big change with a number of uncertainties while we got integrated into the larger company and got inducted into the established ways of working and behaving. The years that followed saw a very frequent restructuring in the organisation and during that period of time, I lost it again and my stammer came back with full force.

I did what I knew best; I put my defences up, buckled down and focused on becoming an expert in my field of expertise. For years I worked as a pre-sales Solutions Architect working on multi-million pound bids and I became really good at it. People around me got made redundant but my in-tray was always full. I conformed to all the standards, processes and templates and brought my insight and skills to the solutions that I developed.

But, I was deeply unhappy as my acute stammering had come back. This meant that although all the ideas, solutions, models and slides came from me, I never got to present them myself. I would take hours to explain them to someone else who will then take my work and present it. Other people told the stories written by me but I never got to tell my stories myself.

One day, one of the bids that landed in my in-tray was a request for proposal for outsourcing of IT applications development and maintenance for a FTSE 100 utility company. It was a highly competitive multi-million pound bid.

We were facing some tough competition from a major Indian IT Services company, and, even after working day and night for three weeks, Alison, the sales director, was of the view that the commercials were not stacking up, we would not win the contract and we would have to come up with a radical and innovative solution to the whole thing.

We were all tired after three gruelling weeks, and a

bit deflated that we still don't have the winning solution. I left for home early and went to sleep straightaway mulling over various options in my head.

Overnight, I came up with a brilliant idea – to use a completely different approach for service transition and delivery. I got up and redid the full solution, delivery approach, resource model and commercial model. The numbers started to stack up and were well within the range given by Alison. I emailed all the new material to the team by early morning and went to sleep again.

In the afternoon, when I reached the office and saw Alison, she was clearly convinced that we have a winning bid now.

We had only two weeks left before the presentations to the customer. Alison asked me if I would like to present the solution to the customer team. All in all, it will be about 30 participants. I refused as I could not because of my stammer.

Over the next few days Alison lined up a few people who I would explain the solution to, and they would then present. This was a radical approach never tried before and no one was able to bring it to life and stand up to scrutiny during mock presentations.

There was a week left to go, and Alison approached me and told me that she had decided that she will only go forward with this bid if I, myself, would present it to the customer. After all, it was all my work and my ideas and only I could do justice. She had full confidence that I could do it and she would line up the full senior management team in the sector to give me support, coaching and as many practice sessions as I needed.

On the one hand I was terrified of the prospect of presenting to 30 odd strangers but on the other hand, I felt elated by the confidence Alison and the senior management team had shown in me, knowing fully well my limitations.

So, it all started, with just one week left to go, I was given a meeting room just to myself and a projector to take home if I wanted to practice. I practised all day in the room and twice a day the senior management team would gather for my mock presentation practice.

I was not cutting it, I would stammer heavily in every practice session. Participants showed a lot of patience, empathised with me, kept a brave face and told me that they believe I can do it. I was given a lot of encouragement but there was nothing anybody could do. My presentation improved over a period of time as I memorised most of what I needed to say and just said it, but the performance was highly variable. For a few minutes, it went well and then one slight stammer would start a vicious cycle of self-doubt and I would suddenly go into an acute stammer.

One day before the presentation day, we had a rehearsal presentation in the morning which was no better, a few changes were agreed and we decided to have a final practice during lunch time. Even the final try was no better, in fact, it got worse and we decided to call it a day and meet at the presentation venue the next morning for the presentation.

I came back home completely gutted, with a huge burden on my shoulders of the scary thought of making a mess in the presentation tomorrow and being the centre of humiliation and defeat. I would let Alison and the team down who had so much wanted me to succeed and had put their trust and faith in me, not to mention the loss of a multi-million-pound business to the company.

I got up just before 2'o clock in the morning, set up

the projector in the living room and gave it one final try. I needed an audience, so I decided to wake up my son Tushar, who was about 15 years old at the time, and asked if he would help in the trial presentation by being my audience.

I started to present, started to stammer and could not hack it. In desperation, I pulled out the extendable antenna of our house phone and started using it as a presentation stick to help me give confidence. It helped a bit but I still could not present successfully.

At this point, I looked at Tushar for help and he asked me to stop presenting. In a very calm and thoughtful voice he said "Dad, you are doing it all wrong. It is clear that you know your stuff as you are the one who created it. But you are trying to read the slides in a formal and corporate way, you are not feeling it. I cannot see any emotion, passion or feelings when you are trying to read through the slides. You are constrained by the format, the layout, and the corporate buzzwords on the slides. They are not yours, but the underlying thinking is yours. It all comes across as made up, it is not you, your innocence and purity of thought do not show through."

He asked me to put the slides up but not read the slides, instead explain in my own words the challenge, the solution, the approach and why I thought that this solution was the best solution in the world. If he wanted to read the slides, they were up there for him to read.

I got it instantly, I had put all sorts of constraints around me, I was holding my original thoughts back and was manufacturing the words that would fit within a corporate culture, would align with my company's positioning, would conform to the brand and company values. The originality and innocence of my thoughts were lost.

I sat down for few minutes, eyes closed and went back to the moment when the original idea came to me overnight and I had worked on it through the night. Why I thought it was a great idea and how I thought it would all work. I watched it like a movie in my head.

I got up and started again. This time I would turn to each slide, look at the heading and then turn to Tushar and explained my own thoughts in my own words. My words were better than the slides, I spoke for 45 minutes and finished the presentation without a single stammer. It was surreal, we practised until 6 in the morning. I was filled with confidence, content with myself and was very clear in my mind what I was going to do. I had rediscovered my innocence and I was not going to let go of it this time.

The presentation was due to start at 8:30 and we were supposed to reach there by 7:30 to do one final rehearsal with Alison. It snowed heavily that night, the roads were clogged and I did not arrive in the car park until 8:00. Alison was waiting for me in the car park in the snow with her eyes firmly on the road waiting for me to arrive. She told me later on that at one point she thought I would not come at all.

As soon as I arrived, Alison rushed towards me wanting to have a discussion and to check if I was OK. I asked her to take me to the presentation room as I needed to do something very important. While showering, getting ready and driving I had worked out five key questions which I thought I would be asked after the presentation. I knew how I needed to answer these but I needed to lay my thoughts out on a piece of paper.

By the time we reached the presentation room, we had just 20 minutes left. I started drawing on the flip charts and started creating supporting diagrams and charts for those five questions. I asked Alison to help me out and stick those flip charts with diagrams onto the walls at the front of the room. Alison was confused as to what I was trying to do and wanted to discuss it. I said no discussion please I am very clear what I am doing just please help me set up the equipment and flip charts. I will not let you down.

People arrived, the room became full of strangers, I was still adding bits to the flip charts I had created, as the wait and silence just before the start of the presentation freaks me out. So, I needed to make sure I was submerged in my original thought process and did not lose my innocence in this daunting formal corporate environment.

Alison started with a corporate introduction, looked at me to see if I was ready, I nodded and she introduced me and invited me to the podium to present.

I thanked Alison and looked at the audience and said "What Alison gracefully forgot to tell you is that I stammer. But, for today, let us just focus on why this solution is the best solution for you". There was silence. "And" pointing to the telescopic phone antenna in my hand, I said "sorry about this but thankfully the phone is still working". There was laughter and the audience was ready to hear what I had to say.

And I started, Alison was switching the slides for me and I just focused on explaining the whole thought process behind the solution, approach, how we would resource it and how we would mitigate risks and why it was the best solution ever. I spoke for 45 minutes, did not stammer even once, took a glass of water and invited questions.

At this point I could see Alison's beaming face and could not help getting the feeling that I was like a little child performing on the stage, filled with honesty, originality, passion and innocence and the audience were like parents of children in the school and each and everyone wanted me to be successful in this performance. Just like they do when a group of children are performing on the school stage.

The questions came and, for another 45 minutes, I answered each of them in detail with the help of my telescopic phone antenna and the flip charts that I had already prepared.

It was a memorable moment. The presentation was over and a number of managers approached me, gave me a warm handshake and thanked me for such a brilliant and informative session full of passion and wished me every success in my future.

As soon as everyone left, Alison lifted me up and twirled me around in joy with tears pouring down her eyes.

We reached back at our base office in Reading and the news had already reached there, walking through the office floor to my desk, numerous people approached me, shook my hand, congratulated me and told me how proud and happy they were.

They were really happy for me, but, in addition, I guess everyone misses the childhood innocence they once had, I had rediscovered it and they were seeing themselves in me.

That day, I had broken all the norms and did not care about the rules, the templates, the accepted norms, behaviours and conventions. I just did what I felt was right and everyone deep inside them always wanted to be able to do that.

This was a turning point in my career.

Over the years that followed, I was really fortunate to get help from a number of very senior people in the company.

Elaine Baker coached me for three years on how to be an effective leader and how to create high performing teams. From David Patterson, I learnt how to have the courage to say and do the right things. John Gibson gave me personal coaching sessions on how to think like a CEO. Steve Weston always rescued me whenever I landed myself into trouble and I learnt invaluable skills in problem-solving from him. Alan

Oliver took the biggest leap of faith in me and gave me my biggest break of my career of managing a multimillion pound business unit with close to 600 people and transforming it over the next 12 months.

All of this came because I eliminated my self-imposed constraints, rediscovered my passion and innocence and all these people perhaps saw their own success in my success.

EXERCISE

This is the same exercise as step-5. This time focus on your limiting beliefs and constraints that are stopping you from moving forward. Remember, your fears are self-imposed and your constraints are imposed by others around you.

> What are top five things, most important for your success, that you are not doing?
>
> What are the top five reasons that you are not doing what you should be doing?
>
> What is that one limiting belief that gives you a feeling that you are tied in shackles and desperate to become free?

.

09 STEP-7: EXECUTE - BECOME A PROLIFIC PRODUCER

"Ideas are ten a penny. Execution is everything. Those who execute, create real and enduring value for the society and those who don't, simply pontificate."

You have now completed steps one to six. You are now in the final and the most important step. Let us summarise what you have achieved so far:

ENVISION

Have a vision and set yourself an audacious goal, clearly articulate it to yourself and to others.

You have worked out what you are passionate about. You have clarity on your vision and you can clearly articulate it to yourself and to others around you. You can see yourself making a big positive impact in a few years' time. You are ready to champion your cause.

ENABLE

Find the time, tools and resources to enable yourself to pursue your goals.

You know that you need to become an expert in your chosen subject or field. You need to stay current on your subject and develop a habit of lifelong learning. We live in a world today where there is an abundance of resources. In order to achieve your goals, if you require certain resources, someone has already got them. You just need to seek them out.

ENERGISE

Discover your value mountain to unleash your internal energy, energise yourself and those around you

You have worked out how to become highly aware of your own self. You understand and leverage your strengths, and you are aware of your weaknesses. You have discovered your value mountain and learnt how to energise yourself by watching your own movie.

EMPOWER

Identify and remove your self-imposed constraints, fears and inhibitions and empower yourself.

You have empowered yourself by confronting your fears and eliminating your constraints.

You are ready to go. You are ready to go to the final step:

EXECUTE

Consistently produce outcomes that are meaningful for you and those around you.

This is the final and most important step. You need to execute, produce and create. Produce a lot. Prolific beats perfect. You are known by what you produce and what you create. You will fade into irrelevance as soon as you stop producing and creating. You are only as good as the quality of your last output.

Look at any famous or successful person around you. They are successful because of the output they have produced, not the other way around.

Steven Spielberg has produced or directed close to 60 movies.

Amitabh Bachchan has appeared in close to 180 movies

JK Rowling has written at least 25 books

What separates the successful leader from the unsuccessful leader? Why is it that some succeed and others fail? There have been thousands of books written and seminars given to answer that question, but when it comes down to it, there are some who take action and execute and some who don't. Those who do, succeed.

Revisit your plan and make sure that your plan requires you to produce something of value regularly and consistently. Without execution, a vision is nothing more than a dream. Ideas are plentiful. It is the execution that makes the difference.

Take small steps in order to leapfrog. Get small wins under your belt. Do it consistently so that each win builds upon the last one.

Leapfrogging is not one leap; it is a series of leaps.

So, don't stop producing outcomes that are meaningful for you and those around you- outcomes, which support your cause and your passion. Become a prolific producer.

It will not be easy. You will find it difficult. Every time you come across a mental block, go back to the basics. Revisit why you are doing what you are doing. Rekindle your passion and remember the cause you are championing.

Remember that what you do will have an impact on people around you. When you are successful, it will inspire others around you to take the leap as well.

If you follow these steps, it does not matter what industry you are in, what organisation you are working for, what career you are pursuing; you will leapfrog in your career.

The secret is that if you do it right, your definition of career will change.

EXERCISE

I think, just get on and do it. Create a plan and start executing today!

10 WHY IT IS THE WAY IT IS AND WHAT DO WE DO ABOUT IT

"Prior to the industrial revolution, we were all entrepreneurs. After the Information Revolution, we will all be entrepreneurs. The time has come to harness the individual creativity, passion and individuality because these are the only things that cannot be automated."

You have now gone through the LEAP method and no doubt you will try and implement all or some of the steps to achieve your purpose, vision and goal.

It will not be easy, the transformation is never easy. You will come across situations where you feel that the environment around you is holding you back. This chapter will explain why the work environment is the way it is and how the two opposite forces of new and old are creating a crossroad. It will help you to successfully navigate through this situation and will explain what you can do about it and how you can be part of the revolution which changes the word of work for better.

The current business framework in the corporate world has its origin almost 200 years ago as part of the first industrial revolution. The strict top-down hierarchy focused on repeatability, processes, compliance and conformity aims to maximise efficiency and produce identical widgets at a mass scale. The tenure and expertise in a particular process dictated superiority, compensation and power.

For years, we have developed techniques for analysing and segmenting staff into various cohorts. And then describing the characteristics, strengths and weaknesses of these generalist cohorts. Then we set about finding the most effective ways of managing these generalist cohorts. It suited us. People moved from farming the fields to factories and then to offices. Corporate efficiency and profitability depended on lowering the cost of production of the individual widget by mass production, uniformity and conformity.

Most of the components of the system were designed to create boxes and put people in those boxes. Rigid job descriptions were geared towards the functional aspect of work rather than creativity, passion and values.

It is now grossly unsuited for the knowledge economy. Knowledge workers do not need to be managed. They need to be led, nurtured and individually respected.

The world today is full of potential never seen

before. You can live or work anywhere you want. You can learn about anything you want. You can engage with a number of people at just the touch of a button. Google democratised information. Smartphones democratised technology. Platforms such as Amazon and eBay have democratised access to markets and consumers. Yet, we become conditioned to conformity to the current system of how the world of work operates and fail to exploit this tremendous potential.

The next revolution will not be based on automation, mass production, segmentation or controlled execution. It will be based on harnessing the individual potential, creativity and passion of thousands and millions of micro-entrepreneurs.

CONDITIONED TO CONFORMITY

Let us talk about a typical example and hopefully, this will resonate with some of my readers:

We decided that we need to recruit some fresh talent into our department. We have operated this way for the last 30 years and business has been doing well. But, recently we have been facing a relentless onslaught from a number of disrupters in our industry. We need someone with new thinking. Someone with fresh ideas. Someone who is not afraid to challenge the established practices. Someone with passion and courage. Someone who will become a catalyst for change.

We interview 20 people and finally find the one person we were looking for.

Becky came across as passionate, caring for social

and community causes. She had analytical abilities and fresh ideas. She was not afraid to challenge and ask the questions.

She was the new Millennial. Perfect. We make an offer and she accepted.

We were happy with our find and we eagerly wait for Becky to join our team.

On day one we ask Becky to go through a week-long corporate induction process. She is introduced to the managers in the department who have worked here for a number of years. We make sure she goes through our brand guidelines and is on message. We point her to the notice board which proudly displays local rules of the office including a prominent list of Do's and Don'ts.

During her formal and informal meetings with various people in the department, we make sure that she is fully aware of the likes and dislikes of each of the manager.

We ask Becky to read through and sign our use of social media policy. We ask her to attend an online tutorial on Health and Safety policy. We then take her through one-day training to induct her on how to make the best use of our company intranet and where she can find processes and forms on all aspects of working in our company.

We also inform her that she will have a probation period and an annual appraisal cycle. She will need to agree her objectives with her manager at the beginning of the year and her end of the year bonus will be dependent on meeting those objectives.

The promotions cycle runs on a yearly basis and if she does well she will be looking to become a manager in about 10 years. The promotions are also dependent on a suitable vacant position becoming available.

Occasionally when Becky challenged our processes and procedures we suggested that these are long-established processes and she needs to first settle in and understand the company business and culture before making an observation.

In about thirty days, we conditioned her into our way of operating. All the good qualities that we recruited her for have been suppressed.

Her core that we recruited her for is now hidden beneath a number of layers that we helped create.

She feels handicapped.

Let us now see what Becky would have brought to the table before we conditioned her.

> She is motivated by meaning. She is interested in discovering, why is she doing what she is doing and how does it help her customers, society and environment.
>
> She is not afraid to share her opinions and ideas, nor challenge those of her superiors.
>
> She prefers a cross-functional way of working that cuts across the constraints of rank.
>
> She would like an equal relationship with her manager and others around her as she believes everyone has an inherent potential to add value.
>
> She believes that social media helps her to stay connected and highly aware. It helps her to think and form views and opinions. It is not a

productivity sucker.

She does not agree to just do things in a certain way just because this is how it has always been done. It is her nature to challenge the status quo.

She is task and output oriented, not time oriented. So, she cannot figure out why she needs to be physically in the office 9 to 5. She places higher importance on the value she delivers to the organisation rather than time spent in the office.

She has a hunger for learning and solving problems. Becoming an expert on a process and repeatedly undertaking the same process every day does not inspire her.

Beyond understanding how to perform a task, she wants to understand why and what problem we are trying to solve? How can it be done better?

She wants to know how well she is doing today rather than waiting for the end of the year appraisal ritual. She wants constant feedback and appreciation to fuel her hunger for being the best she can be.

She prefers a less formal, output-oriented approach to work and believes in having fun at the workplace to find business value in bonding with teammates and taking a break for the creative inspiration.

Becky wants to work the way she lives, enjoy it, add value to herself and others around her, solve complex problems using simple and fun solutions and feel accomplished. Everyday.

We tell her not to think too much and just do what she is told to do as our corporate vision, values and strategic plan displayed prominently all over the place have already figured all of it out!

THE ENVIRONMENT

Let us now look at 'The Manager', Martin. He probably comes from the Boomer generation. He has spent years on the slow climb onto the corporate ladder. He has spent years becoming an expert in his functional area. He has also developed valuable skills in working with the corporate machinery.

Martin understands the politics and what makes people progress in their careers. He has a mortgage, a car loan, and kids in private school or college. When he was younger, he had a dream and passion, but now he is not really passionate about what he does but he does it as it pays the bills.

Martin has learnt conformity. He has learnt how to meet the expectations of others around him. For him, tenure equals superiority, influence, pay and responsibility. As far as he is concerned, you need to do your time, as he has done, before you challenge and 'innovate'.

He is correct in his own way, yet, he is a product of industrialisation and corporatisation of our society.

Multiply this by the hundreds of managers and senior managers you see around you and you will see the problem.

This is the environment which stops you from achieving your full potential. You cannot change the environment. It is ingrained in the culture built over decades. Trying to change this will only frustrate you. This will not change until the Boomers start to retire and Millennials start to move into management and influential roles within the corporate world. This will take time but will happen.

Take for example the use of Open-source softwares. These softwares are created by communities of people spread around the world who are passionate about technology and solving complex problems by using simple technology. The software is free to use and improve upon by anyone in the world.

The good quality Open-source software has existed for decades. Open-source was a revolution in itself by people who were frustrated by the closed, costly and constrained offering by big software vendors. Some of you must have heard about Unix (an operating system) and Wordpress (a software to create websites), both are examples of Open-source software. Some of this software is far superior to commercially available software by big vendors.

Until a few years ago, corporates did not use the Open-source software as it was developed by 'geeks'. They considered it inferior and unreliable. The IT managers felt that if they use commercial software from big vendors and things went wrong, they can't be blamed for failures of those projects. After all, one does not get fired for using Microsoft or Oracle as their forebearers did not get fired for buying IBM.

Things are changing rapidly now, corporates and even government organisations are increasingly using the Open-source software in their operational and mission-critical systems. One of the reasons for this change is that the 'geeks' who championed Open-source are slowly moving up the corporate ladder. They have started to occupy influential positions in IT departments of companies across the globe and are actively championing the Open-source revolution. The 'old guard' who found comfort with big software vendors and never rated Open-source software has started to retire or give way.

Clearly, there are exceptions. There are a number of very good visionary and transformative managers and leaders around us.

Some are reformers, tirelessly fighting the established system and norm. Some will help and support you covertly and will bend or side-step the process whenever they can to support you. But, these are a minority.

I was fortunate to have really good managers and I also actively sought to work with reformers. But, at some point, all of them felt helpless in front of the political ecosystem and established norms within the company.

I felt that they had the deep desire to do the right thing but at times some problems became too difficult to solve and some battles too difficult to fight. The establishment feels threatened and people will close rank. It was better to accept defeat and support status quo.

POWER OF YOU

You clearly cannot wait years for Boomers to retire and hope everything will be as you expect it to be. You should not wait.

You think that you are not achieving your full potential. Your dreams seem to be distant. The world around you does not understand you. You have little or no influence on how things are done in your company and how decisions are made. You don't believe that businesses really care about the social causes that you are so passionate about. You don't feel that you belong. You have this niggling feeling of getting left behind. It frustrates you.

You are an ordinary person. You want to make a difference to the world around you. You want to have a sense of accomplishment. You want to feel fulfilled. You have ideas and energy that if deployed effectively can make a big difference. You care about the society and community. You want to be part of the revolution that redistributes wealth and brings equality. You want to be successful and help others around you to be part of that success.

You don't need to change the environment around you. You need to reawaken yourself to who you truly are. You need to become highly aware of your strengths and weaknesses. You need to leverage your strengths. You do not need to try to hide or fix your weaknesses, those are part of who you are. Bring clarity about your passions and goals. Then re-energise yourself by recognising your past successes and wins. Recognise what you truly care about, what drives you and what makes you sad.

We care too much about what other people think of us. We are constrained by the accepted norms of behaviour. We try and meet the expectations of others. We try and be what others expect us to be and in that process, our self goes and hides in the background.

You need to learn to identify your self-imposed constraints and free yourselves from these. You do not need to meet others expectations from you. You need to identify your true self, your own drivers and passions and try and be who you truly are. You do not need to prove anything to anybody but to yourself.

You need to unleash your inner power and become your own champion.

SUMMARY

The world of work has not kept pace with the socio-economic changes driven by unparalleled technological advances over the last decade.

Advanced automation has meant that the nature of jobs is changing. The future of work will be influenced by the premise that robots can perform any task except the ones that require fundamental human potential driven by passion, creativity, compassion, vision and values.

The current environment does not allow the

individual potential to be fully unleashed.

If all of us are driven by the passion and a deep desire to do the right thing about the issues that we care about, the environment around us will change. We can become a champion of our own cause. We will be part of a revolution, led by ordinary champions.

There has not been a better time for this revolution. The internet has made the world a smaller place. It has given ordinary people a voice and a reach. A reach that cuts across boundaries of age, language, culture and nation.

The Millennials are already making a big impact on this world. This generation will bring profound change. The new heroes are those who pursue their passion and a cause. They have a face recognised and loved by millions around the world. Elon Musk of Tesla is a brand in himself far bigger than the CEO of General Motors.

11 SIX COMMON MISTAKES

*"Remembering that I'll be dead soon is the most
important tool I've ever encountered to help me make
the big choices in life. Because almost everything - all
external expectations, all pride, all fear of
embarrassment or failure - these things just fall away in
the face of death, leaving only what is truly important."*

-Steve Jobs

We all go through a dip in our working life or our career,
when nothing seems to be going our way. Some of us
do get left behind, and some of us keep on charging
ahead.

So, the question is why is it the way it is?

If you are currently going through a dip, you
probably think that you are not achieving your full

potential. You have this niggling feeling of getting left behind. You also think this is because of the environment around you, your company or your manager. You feel that there is nothing you can do except to carry on or look for another job.

You are probably wrong.

Yes, environment plays a big part. Environment dictates performance. The good environment promotes achievement. The bad environment creates mental blocks. When mental blocks are created we lose our rationality and clarity of thinking. Our performance dips.

Chances are that there are certain thinking mistakes that you are making subconsciously. This incorrect thinking is influencing you to take wrong actions. Your thinking and actions together are creating the problems that you are facing. If you put your mind to it, you can easily turn things around and you will no longer have a feeling of getting left behind.

In this chapter, I will try and explain the mistakes you are making, the problems these mistakes are creating and how you can turn the situation to your advantage with a little bit of self-improvement.

GIVING UP

"I realised early on that success was tied to not giving up. Most people in this business gave up and went on to other things. If you simply didn't give up, you would outlast the people who came in on the bus with you."

– Harrison Ford

We think that we are not as capable as others around us or we have a handicap. We think we are not a strategic thinker. So, we don't set bigger goals for ourselves and don't try and visualise the possibilities in front of us. As a result, we continue to operate at a level that is way below our own potential. We give up trying.

Rose was a teaching assistant. She was very good with children but had a speech impediment. She always wanted to become a teacher but was not confident she could become one due to her speech impediment. Due to this reason, for years, she did not try to obtain a teaching degree.

One day, she set herself a goal to become a teacher and decided to apply for a place in the local university to obtain a teaching degree. It took her three years to clear numerous hurdles and she obtained a place for a teaching degree at her local university. She became one of the best teachers in her school despite the speech impediment.

My best advice is to start by setting simple goals and achieve them. Get small successes under your belt to build your self-confidence and self-discipline. It could be as simple as getting up early in the morning, running for 30 minutes or cooking a new dish every week, whatever you fancy.

The trick is to do what you enjoy doing, set simple goals to start with and make sure you achieve them. Once you have built enough self-confidence, then it is time to set yourself an audacious goal and set about achieving it. Don't give up.

UNDERVALUING OURSELVES

"The true meaning of courage is to be afraid, and then, with your knees knocking and your heart racing, to step out anyway—even when that step makes sense to nobody but you. I know that's not easy. But making a bold move is the only way to truly advance toward the grandest vision the universe has for you."

— Oprah Winfrey

We think that we have not had many successes in life compared to others around us. We have not achieved much in life to be proud of. So, we don't put in thinking to discover our own value mountain and lose our ability to think. As a result of this, we hugely undervalue ourselves in our own eyes.

Peter, who had a very good academic and sports performance during his school years started to severely underperform during his university degree and lost self-confidence and self-esteem. He and people close to him started to believe that he had developed a mental disorder and was put on medication to no effect. He then went through a process of re-discovering his successes and achievements during previous years. As a result of this, he became re-energised helping him gain his self-confidence. After this, his performance dramatically improved.

Everyone is standing on their own mountain of value, they just can't see it. You should try watching the highlights of your life as a movie, the simple successes you have already achieved, the joy you brought to others and to yourself and the passions that you had. When you were a baby, learning to walk and speak was a success. You just forgot about it and now you need to learn to visualise it. Once you have discovered your own value mountain, visualise your goal and go forward with full courage.

FORGETTING WHO WE TRULY ARE

"I believe there's an inner power that makes winners or losers. And the winners are the ones who really listen to the truth of their hearts."

— Sylvester Stallone

We think that we need to operate within the constraints imposed by the environment and others around us. So, we stop being ourselves. We work to meet other people's expectations and approval under self-imposed constraints and fears. As a result, we suppress our own passions, values and inner strengths and operate at a suboptimal level.

Mike had a severe speech impediment and was asked to present an outsourcing proposal to a high-profile audience. Mike had himself developed the ideas and solutions in the proposal but was not confident of his ability to present in a formal corporate environment, norms and format. Mike went through a process of removing all constraints and doubts from his mind and delivered a very successful presentation in his own words, format and using his inner voice. This was a turning point and Mike went on to become a very successful transformational leader in his organisation.

If you are facing this problem, the best advice is to be yourself, find your inner passion, your innocence and your voice, and express them. People like honesty and hate manufactured presentations. Try and be a child performing on a school stage with a room full of parents and every parent wants this child to perform well, as they are moved by the innocence and honesty of the child. If you persevere and don't let external constraints and fear dictate your actions, you will finally succeed.

HIDING OUR WEAKNESSES

"I view the accident (and my resulting disability) as a blessing because without it I would be one amongst the million women who dance."

– Sudha Chandran – internationally acclaimed dancer

We are worried about what people would think if they found out our shortcomings or handicaps. So, rather than overcoming the weaknesses or acknowledging the handicaps, we put in tremendous effort to mask them from others. As a result, the effect of the handicap intensifies and we don't come across as genuine and trustworthy. We forget that our handicap is possibly what makes us unique.

Martin had an acute stammer and was always fearful of people finding out that he stammered. The fear of being found out meant that he avoided the situations where he needed to speak with people and when he spoke his fear of stammer will only exaggerate the problem. This became a self-fulfilling cycle as he put tremendous effort into hiding this problem from others. Martin went through a process of learning to acknowledge and accept his handicap publicly to remove this fear and actively sought opportunities where he needed to speak to people. As soon as the fear was removed, Martin went on to recover rapidly from his handicap and has had a very successful professional career.

If you have handicaps, don't hide them but acknowledge them, everyone has handicaps, so you are not alone. If you are fearful of something, confront it, do more of it till it is no longer a fear.

NOT SEEKING OUT RESOURCES

"I believe you can speak things into existence"

-Jay-Z, Decoded

We think that the things that we really want to achieve are probably too ambitious and we will not get resources, time, support or help. So, we don't challenge the status quo and don't seek out resources to help us to fulfil our own dreams. As a result of this, despite having set a credible goal, and having the energy and willingness to succeed, we are not able to achieve our goals.

Tom, with an economics degree, became an investment banker. The job was well-paying, had long hours but was boring and not fulfilling. Tom spotted some real opportunities to disrupt current inefficient industries and was craving to be a tech entrepreneur but this goal seemed a bit too impossible. Coming from an ordinary family background he did not have access to the right network, coaching, mentoring and funding support. Tom set about enrolling for some technology courses, started to write his blogs, applied to join a start-up incubator, got introduced to influential people in the industry and went on to create a successful tech startup in the commercial real estate space.

If you really want to achieve something, someone already has the resources that you need. It is a question of finding them. Meet people; build networks, relationships, alliances and partnerships. They will be more than happy to help you if you are passionate about your vision, demonstrate energy and single-minded focus to achieve it.

BECOMING IRRELEVANT

"Success is a lousy teacher. It seduces smart people into thinking they can't lose"

– Bill Gates

We think that we have done something for years, we have become good and successful at it, so we should just continue to do it rather than learning something new. So, we stop learning new skills, stop stretching ourselves and don't reinvent ourselves. As a result, soon we find ourselves becoming irrelevant and get left behind.

Madonna has experienced sustained success over three decades. Madonna achieved this sustained success because she is a consistent producer of exemplary outputs that are in tune with the time and changing expectations of the audiences. She has this unique ability to adapt to the changes demanded by time and she has constantly reinvented herself to stay relevant for much longer than anyone else in her profession.

The trick is consistent execution, production of output, lifelong learning, innovation and reinvention. When you achieve a small goal, don't rest. Set another goal, improve upon what you did before and continue to produce meaningful and improved outcomes in an incremental fashion. If you are successful in doing something, learn something new; learn it fast, so you can continue to be successful.

SUMMARY

When you apply the LEAP method to your own situation and still feel that you are not moving forward, think about what mistakes you are making subconsciously which if rectified can improve the results for you.

There are six examples in this chapter and there are plenty more out there. You just need to find one that is applicable to your situation and then work on rectifying it.

Remember, success is not instant, it is cumulative. It is not given, it is earned.

Most important of all it is not easy, it requires determination, courage and drive.

ACKNOWLEDGMENTS

Amazing things can be achieved when people come together to champion a common cause. I have always believed that if you have a vision and you articulate this vision with a passion and commitment that it deserves, people from all walks of life will rally around you to help support that vision.

I have been fortunate to have numerous people help me bring this book to publication in a record six months.

I would like to sincerely thank:

My wife, Rashmi, for providing support and encouragement throughout the process as all the work was carried out during weekends and late nights.

Elaine Baker and Norbert Lieckfeldt, who agreed to write the Foreword for the book.

David Patterson, who was always there whenever I faced a dilemma and he agreed to review and final proofread the book. He has sharp eyes!

David Willcox, who provided his trademark cartoons

and illustrations and read every single one of my articles.

Ranjan Jha, who created the elegant design of the cover of the book.

Catherine Gutsell for assuming the charge as the editor of the book and providing invaluable feedback throughout the various drafts of the book.

Mohit Talwar, for sticking with me throughout the journey from initial ideas, scribbles and notes to the full book. He reviewed every idea and draft and provided much-needed encouragement during the whole process.

Maxy Patel, who provided a much-needed challenge to my intellectual and rational way of thinking. The book needed a soul in addition to a method. She greatly influenced the honest and spiritual flavour in my writing that was essential for connecting with the hearts and minds of my readers.

Sean Jones, Orla Cummins and Alex Fiorello for religiously attempting every exercise at the end of each chapter and providing invaluable review feedback

Judy Holliday, Steve Weston, Dr Volker Lanninger and Abby Reyes, who invested their personal time in reviewing the various drafts.

Sonan Nair and Vishal Nair for acting as the very first focus group to test the ideas in a Millennials context.

Special thanks to Nitika Popli, who read all my blogs, articles and drafts and provided invaluable reader feedback over the last five months.

Daniel Priestley, entrepreneur, best-selling author and international speaker, who encouraged me to write the book and even came up with its title.

Lucy McCarraher, Managing Editor of Rethink Press for providing invaluable coaching and guidance throughout the process.

When I spoke to my friends and colleagues about the book, I was overjoyed with the encouragement and support. So much so that not a single task in the creation of this book has been paid for. Every effort for all aspects of the book has been provided on a voluntary basis by these amazing people.

It is only fitting that all proceeds from the sale of this book are donated to The British Stammering Association, a registered charity in the UK.

ABOUT THE AUTHOR

Manoj is a transformation expert with a technology background. He helps organisations deliver outstanding results by creating high performing teams and helping individuals to outperform themselves.

Over the years, working with blue chip organisations such as Tata, Scottish Life Assurance, Steria, Fujitsu and now Hays Plc, he has delivered numerous transformation projects at a global scale. In an environment where more than two-thirds of IT projects fail, Manoj achieved a one hundred percent success rate and is now providing advice to other senior leaders on how to achieve similar successes.

The key ingredients of this consistent success have been transforming people, not technology.

You can keep in touch with Manoj on:

LinkedIn: www.linkedin.com/in/manoj-agarwal-uk/

Email: info@OrdinaryChampions.life
Websites: www.OrdinaryChampions.life
                 www.theLEAPbooks.com

WHAT NEXT?

After reading this book, you may feel inspired to take charge of your career and shape your own destiny. You may find the following resources useful:

Some interesting and insightful books:
"Good to Great" by Jim Collins
"Built to Last" by Jim Collins and Jerry Porras
"Straight from the Gut" by Jack Welch
"Entrepreneur Revolution" by Daniel Priestley
"Little Wins" by Paul Lindley

You can also visit the Ordinary Champions website to access more resources and articles to help your pursuit at:
www.OrdinaryChampions.life

If you feel that you are passionate about this subject and would like to write about it or contribute to the discussion, just visit the "Become one of our Authors" page on the above website and submit your draft article. We would be very happy to have you as part of the team.

If you liked the book, it would be great if you could submit a review on Amazon. If you send a screenshot of that review to info@OrdinaryChampions.life, we will send you a LEAP Scorecard. This will help you self-score your progress through the LEAP method.

Thanks for reading Ordinary Champions.

Printed in Great Britain
by Amazon